THE LOST
CROWN

THE LOST CROWN

What Scripture Says About
Our Rewards in Heaven

J. WILBUR CHAPMAN

We enjoy hearing from our readers. Please contact us at www.anekopress.com/questions-comments with any questions, comments, or suggestions.

Contents

I am coming quickly; hold firmly to what you have, so that no one will take your crown. – Revelation 3:11

Preface

After much prayer and thoughtful consideration of the subject, this book is published with the hope that it may be both a warning and an inspiration to all who may take the time to read what is written here.

God forbid that any of us should miss our crown at the great day of awards! God grant that we may all receive the full reward!

No claim is made to literary excellence, but it is claimed:

First, that in the presentation of these subjects to my own people, they were kind enough to say that they had been greatly awakened.

Secondly, that these sermons, as far as they appeal

to the unsaved, have been used by God to lead many to decide for Christ. To Him be all the praise!

The two companion books, *And Peter* and *Kadesh-barnea*, have been so graciously received and so widely read that I am encouraged to believe that this book may also be helpful to many.

If one child of God is inspired to better service, and if one poor lost sinner is led to Christ, I will never cease to praise Him for the privilege He has given me of preparing these messages.

J. Wilbur Chapman
Bethany Presbyterian Church, Philadelphia, PA
January 1898

Chapter 1

God's Plan for Us

Not that I have already obtained it or have already become perfect, but I press on so that I may lay hold of that for which also I was laid hold of by Christ Jesus. – Philippians 3:12

God has a plan for every life, and when this plan is realized, there is always in the experience of the believer both joy and peace, blessing and power. If anyone is having an up-and-down Christian experience, hot today and cold tomorrow, near enough to Christ today so that he may almost touch Him, and so far away tomorrow that he questions if he has ever been saved, this is certain evidence that he has not allowed God to work out His plan for him. There is still much work to be accomplished by the Holy Spirit of God.

An experience of unrest dishonors God, and when you find a heart in which there is this unrest and dissatisfaction, you always find a life in which God has not yet finished His work. *Peace I leave with you; My peace I give to you* (John 14:27). That was written for such a person, and it is his inheritance. While it would be a most difficult thing to define peace, yet possibly the best definition would be to take its opposite, and so it would read like this: Peace is the opposite of unrest, confusion, and strife. This blessing is for each of God's children, if they will only claim it.

It is no more disastrous for one's arm to be out of its socket than for one's life to run contrary to the plan of God. Paul evidently had this in mind when he said, *That I may lay hold of that for which also I was laid hold of by Christ Jesus* (Philippians 3:12). It would be no more disastrous for a planet to go swinging out of its orbit than for a life to run contrary to the plan of God. The fact is that our crosses in this world always come to us when our wills run contrary to the will of God. One piece of wood placed over another and running in the contrary direction always makes a cross. Our peace and joy come to us in this life when our wills run parallel to God's will. Although we may be bound to live in poverty and meet with what this

Our peace and joy come to us in this life when our wills run parallel to God's will.

world calls disaster and failure, if we are perfectly sure that what we are doing is according to God's will, we may say with the apostle Paul, *God causes all things to work together for good* (Romans 8:28).

A High Ideal for Every Life

God has a high ideal for every life, and we only have to read the Scriptures to find this to be true. We find in Romans 1:7 that we are called *saints*; this is our name. We learn in 1 Corinthians 3:9 that we are *God's fellow workers*. We are told in 1 Corinthians 1:9 that it is our privilege to be in fellowship with God's Son. This word *fellowship* is literally "partnership." In Revelation 2:17, God promises to give to us His own *hidden manna* to eat. The world knows nothing of this. It can neither give it nor take it away.

In Psalm 25:14, we have a pledge that God will tell His secrets to us, but it is not to be forgotten that we only tell secrets to those who are near to us. God never gives His secrets to those who are out of fellowship with Him, and everyone is out of fellowship who has any unconfessed or unforgiven sin in his heart. In Philippians 3:20, the conversation, or citizenship, of the child of God is described. It is to be in heaven, from which place we also look for the Savior, the Lord Jesus Christ. In Ephesians 2:10, the entirety of the Christian character is described. We are told that *we are His workmanship*. The word *workmanship* is literally "poem," so that in God's plan, we are all that is complete and beautiful.

We are very sure that we have not attained unto this plan. We are likewise confident that falling short of it, we are not satisfied, and our cry is that of the apostle Paul (Romans 7:24): *Wretched man that I am! Who will set me free from the body of this death?*

We may have God's power. *He has said to me, "My grace is sufficient for you, for power is perfected in weakness." Most gladly, therefore, I will rather boast about my weaknesses, so that the power of Christ may dwell in me* (2 Corinthians 12:9). Let us therefore cease to speak of the presence of the Holy Spirit as an experience and talk about the better Christian life as an "it." Let us remember from now on that Christ is the power of God. To exalt Him, to follow Him, to live His life, and to enthrone Him in our lives is power always, and never can be anything else.

We may have God's rest. *Therefore, let us fear if, while a promise remains of entering His rest, any one of you may seem to have come short of it. For indeed we have had good news preached to us, just as they also; but the word they heard did not profit them, because it was not united by faith in those who heard. For we who have believed enter that rest, just as He has said, "As I swore in My wrath, they shall not enter My rest," although His works were finished from the foundation of the world.* (Hebrews 4:1-3)

It is most significant that in the tenth verse of this fourth chapter of Hebrews we read: *For the one who has entered His rest has himself also rested from his works, as God did from His.* Oh, that we might all learn that it is when we cease to be self-centered and become Christ-centered; when we live lives of unselfishness and therefore for the glory of Christ; when we look up and not in – in a word, it is when we cease from our own works that we enter into God's rest.

We may have God's holiness. *For they disciplined us for a short time as seemed best to them, but He disciplines us for our good, so that we may share His holiness* (Hebrews 12:10). Not infrequently we find Christian people who are afraid of the word *holiness,* yet the Bible has distinctly declared that without holiness no one will see God (Hebrews 12:14). If we

> If we are shutting God out of our lives, then we are depriving ourselves of our birthright as His children.

are shutting Him out of our lives, then we are depriving ourselves of our birthright as His children.

We might sum up God's plan for our lives under three headings:

1. Regeneration

It is God's will for us to be regenerated. *Who were born, not of blood nor of the will of the flesh nor of the will of man, but of God. And the Word became flesh, and dwelt among us, and we saw His glory, glory as of the only begotten from the Father, full of grace and truth* (John 1:13-14).

Regeneration is not a working over of the old nature,

for *that which is born of the flesh is flesh* (John 3:6), and it can never be anything else. It may be educated flesh or cultured flesh, but it is still flesh, and it is displeasing to God. It does not come as the result of reformation, for while reformation may touch a person's present and possibly his future, it has nothing to do with his past sins, which are like the sands of the sea in number. One's surroundings has nothing to do with our passing from death unto life. If our surroundings could save the soul or keep it, Adam would never have fallen, for he lived in paradise. Lot would have been a model citizen, for he lived in the fairest city of the then known world.

Regeneration is God's breathing into man His own life; it is literally being born from above.

2. Sanctification

It is God's will for us to be sanctified. *For this is the will of God, your sanctification* (1 Thessalonians 4:3).

Some people feel very opposed to the idea of sanctification, but it is in God's Word, and it would be good for us to study it and realize it in our experience. To be sanctified is to be separated, and it is certainly the plan of God for His people to be a separated people. While they are in the world, they are to be in no sense *of the world* (John 17:14-16). They are commanded not even to touch that which is unclean (Leviticus 7:21; 2 Corinthians 6:17), and all the old law respecting the Nazarite is a law for the Christian, except that in the New Testament times that law has been intensified by the touch of the living and risen Christ.

If your life is not sanctified, you will live contrary to the will of God.

3. Glorification

It is God's will for us to be ultimately glorified. *The God of all grace, who called you to His eternal glory in Christ, will Himself perfect, confirm, strengthen and establish you* (1 Peter 5:10). *Father, I desire that they also, whom You have given Me, be with Me where I am, so that they may see My glory which You have given Me* (John 17:24).

It is a good thing to turn again and again in this way to the Scriptures in order to find what the plan is that God has marked out for us, and then to check our lives according to this plan to see wherein we have followed it or have failed. If the failure has been severe, it is not necessary for us to go in mourning all day long, for just as a mother forgives the weakness of her child and forgets the many shortcomings, so God has promised again and again in His Word to blot out all our transgressions and to remember them no more against us forever (e.g., Isaiah 43:25).

It is not therefore a question as to whether we can keep from sinning ourselves, for we know that we cannot, but it is entirely a question as to whether Christ can keep us if we will only allow Him to do so. I am certain that one could walk from one corner of the street to the other with Christ so constantly before him that, in his own judgment at

> God has promised again and again in His Word to remember our transgressions no more.

least, he would be overcoming sin during the duration of that short walk. I am perfectly convinced that he could increase his journey by many miles and still be more than conqueror. I am absolutely confident that one could walk the whole day with Christ so vividly before him that it would be peace and joy. And what could be accomplished in one day could be made the course of a person's entire life.

Chapter 2

The Full Reward

The faithful student of the Word of God will find it clearly proven that one may be saved, yet miss in this life very much of the peace and joy of God. After living such a life, he may be ushered into eternity just barely saved, as Paul puts it: *so as through fire* (1 Corinthians 3:15), or as Job describes it: *escaped only by the skin of my teeth* (Job 19:20). This certainly cannot be a very happy outlook, and God throws out danger signals all along the way so that we may turn aside from such unholy living and be kept back from such an inglorious entrance into heaven.

The same student of the Bible will learn that it is possible to enter into God's presence with *fullness of joy* (Psalm 16:11), to be welcomed with the shouts of angels, and to be saluted by the *Well done, good and faithful [servant]* by the Master Himself (Matthew 25:23). Such an entrance into glory is certainly to be desired, and such a joyous experience may be given to every consistent follower of Christ.

After the return of Christ for His church, there is to be a great day of awards, when those who have been faithful will receive recognition at the hands of the Lord Himself in the presence of the assembled hosts in the skies. We can tell just what this reward is to be, yet this needs a word of explanation. We cannot give the exact description of the crowns we will wear, nor can we estimate in human language their value in the opinion of men, but after studying the New Testament, we know that it is to be according to our faith and in proportion to our faithfulness. It is in this way that every child of God may confidently say, "I know what my award is to be." He measured it himself.

> Those who have been faithful will receive recognition at the hands of the Lord Himself.

It is very true that one may stand before God and receive from Him only a measure of reward, and it is likewise true that he might have a greater blessing from the hands of his Master. John speaks about *a full reward* (2 John 1:8), as if there might be a reward that is not complete. This is only too true! However, the opposite is also true, that one may have at that great day at the hands of God Himself *a full reward*.

The purpose of this book is to convince us to lay hold of the promises of God so that our lives may be so shaped according to His will that when that day comes, we will stand before Him with rejoicing and not with sorrow.

A crown is always a symbol of reward. Expressions containing the word are many times used in the New Testament. It is sometimes a *crown of life* (Revelation 2:10), a crown that is *imperishable* (1 Corinthians 9:24-25), a *crown of exultation* or rejoicing (1 Thessalonians 2:19), a *crown of righteousness* (2 Timothy 4:8), and a *crown of glory* (1 Peter 5:4). These names are not given simply for the sake of emphasis, as varying the name might emphasize certain things, but because each crown means a certain kind of reward.

Five Crowns

As far as I have been able to tell, there are only five crowns in the New Testament Scriptures. Every Christian may have one, but oh, the joy of it – every Christian may have five! The message is still sweeter, for if we would receive the five crowns from the hands of our glorified Lord, there would still be something in reserve. We will speak of this later.

The crown of life. Naturally, the crown that should come first in order would be the one mentioned in James 1:12: *Blessed is a man who perseveres under trial; for once he has been approved, he will receive the crown of life which the Lord has promised to those who love Him.*

This crown is also mentioned in Revelation 2:10: *Be faithful unto death, and I will give you the crown of life.*

It was to be given to the church of Smyrna, which suffered the most. I used to read the text as *Be faithful until death*, and I supposed it meant simply that we needed to be faithful during life and that when death came, our responsibility was at an end. However, the word is *unto*, and it means not simply that one should be faithful and willing to suffer for the Master, but to suffer and to die.

This leads me to say that the crown of life is undoubtedly the one to be given to the martyr – not simply the one who has died at the stake, or the woman who has been thrown to the wild beasts that they might devour her, but the one who has suffered in body and mind unknown to fame, but suffered nevertheless, and suffered for the glory of God.

It is likewise the crown that is to be given to the one who is able to do only little things for Christ. So many people seem to think that they can do only little for Christ, and therefore they leave that little undone. This is a most serious error. Jesus said, *To the extent that you did it to one of these brothers of Mine, even the least of them, you did it to Me* (Matthew 25:40). A cup of cold water given in His name (Matthew 10:42), a word of cheer spoken for His glory, or a warm handshake so that He may be exalted in the opinion of men – these little things win the eternal reward.

> A cup of cold water given in His name – these little things win the eternal reward.

So many people are asking, "What can I do to further the cause of Christ, to assist my minister, or to help the church?" If I were to suggest one thing that would be most helpful, it would be to offer unceasing prayer for the spread of Christ's kingdom, and for the outpouring of the Holy Spirit upon the man who preaches Christ at the sacred pulpit. I remember very well when I first became pastor of the church where I now minister. After I had preached my first sermon, and the people had presented themselves to say words of encouragement, an old man came walking down the aisle, leaning upon his staff because of his age, and he said to me, "I am afraid you will make it a failure."

I did not consider that to be much of a word of encouragement, and I very much wished he could have given it to me at another time. Then, looking around the church, he added, "We have always had a man of large experience, and the church is large." Then he came nearer, and said, "But I have made up my mind to help you." I wondered in my own mind what he could do. He then said, "I have determined to pray for you every day while you are the pastor of this church, and I have covenanted with two other men to pray for you."

At this my heart was filled with joy, and I thanked God and took courage, feeling confident from the beginning that He had given me the victory. The three men soon grew to ten, and the ten to fifty, and the fifty to two hundred, until now anywhere from three hundred and fifty to five hundred consecrated men bow their heads in prayer with me every Sunday morning at 9:45, praying God's blessing upon me as I preach, and upon the people as they listen. The most wonderful place in all the world to preach is in a church where the atmosphere is permeated with the petitions of faithful Christians for God's blessing upon His ministers. These are they who, upon the great day of awards, will receive the crown of life. They do little things well, to the glory of God.

The imperishable crown. The second crown in order is the imperishable, or incorruptible, crown. *Everyone who competes in the games exercises self-control in all things. They then do it to receive a perishable wreath, but we an imperishable, . . . but I discipline my body and make it my slave, so that, after I have preached to others, I myself will not be disqualified* (1 Corinthians 9:25, 27).

In this figure of speech, Paul is on the racetrack. He is striving to reach the goal and win the prize. Therefore, this is not a question of life, but is entirely a question of awards. He is not writing to the unregenerate, but to the children of God. He says, *I discipline my body and make it my slave, so that, after I have preached to others, I myself will not be disqualified.* The word *disqualified* in the Greek is literally "disapproved." Paul is teaching that even if he is to win the crown that is imperishable, he must deny himself, he must put forth heroic effort, and he must be faithful until the very end.

This spirit is needed in the church. If the first crown is for the passive Christian, the second is for the enthusiastic follower of Christ, and next to the baptism of the Holy Spirit, the church today needs the baptism of enthusiasm. It is a great mistake for people to allow their prejudices to lead them against the methods of church work upon which God has set His seal. There is a cry today against new methods, and people say the need of the time is for the old methods of our fathers. There is some truth in this, but the trouble with the advocates of this proposition is that they do not make their methods old enough.

We need to go back to Pentecostal methods of *giving*, for in those days the disciples gave all they had. We need to go back to Pentecostal methods of *preaching*, for the early preachers had only two themes in mind: Jesus and the resurrection. We need to go back to Pentecostal *living*, for in the olden times the disciples lived in the expectation that each new day would bring back the Lord Himself, and having this hope in Him, their lives became pure and their testimonies powerful.

Every church should change its method every Sunday if the methods in use do not compel the people to accept the gospel. We have no responsibility for conversion, for the Spirit of God takes care of that; but we do have a tremendous responsibility resting upon us to

> The church is not an end, but is rather a means to an end.

make every man, woman, and child understand that the Son of God died to set them free from the penalty of sin, and that He ever pleads at God's right hand to liberate them from its power. The church is not an end, but is rather a means to an end. If it is considered an end, the membership becomes satisfied with the church in itself – with its preaching, its music, its social standing, and its ability to influence the minds of the people. In all seriousness, I dare to say that such a church will be a curse to a community in the thought of God rather than a blessing. We have this to remember: when considered as a means to an end, the church loses sight of itself and realizes that it is in existence only to bring the message of the gospel to every lost sinner. As long as there is one unsaved soul in the world, God calls His children to carry the message of peace and glad tidings of great joy to that one.

There is a scriptural warrant for this frequent change of method. It is all summed up in one word: until. How long did the father wait for his son? *Until* he returned. How long did the woman search for the lost piece of silver? *Until* she found it. How long did the shepherd look for his sheep? *Until* he had it in his arms and was carrying it back with rejoicing to the fold. How often should we change our methods in the church? *Until* we have a method upon which God will set His seal and to which the Holy Spirit will give His approval, because that method compels the people to hear the gospel and to know that Jesus Christ died to save all mankind.

To the ignorant Peter was willing to be considered ignorant – if only he might save some.

Paul was willing to be considered a fool if only he might better influence people. To the wise he would be wise, to the ignorant he was willing to be considered ignorant, and to the weak he was willing to be considered a man of weakness – if only by all means he might save some (1 Corinthians 9:22). May the Lord God fill the church with this spirit! We could shake the cities and move the world with the power of God, and when the great day of awards comes, simply because we had been earnestly sincere, had counted personal ease as nothing, and had labored incessantly by day and by night, in heat and in cold, we should receive the crown that is incorruptible.

The crown of rejoicing. The third crown is the crown of rejoicing, or exultation. *For who is our hope or joy or crown of exultation? Is it not even you, in the presence of our Lord Jesus at His coming?* (1 Thessalonians 2:19).

When Paul remembers the Thessalonians whom he had won for Christ, he immediately replies, "You are our crown of rejoicing." Therefore, this third form of the reward is properly called the soul winner's crown.

Sadly, some who are born of the Spirit, who have been trained in the Christian church, or could have been, and who have lived all their lives dead in sin will never wear this crown; but it is possible for everybody to receive it from the hands of the Master Himself.

This is the crown that Charles Spurgeon is to wear. It is said that thirteen thousand people joined his church under his ministry, and this was only the beginning of the multitude of others who have been influenced by his life all around the world. It is the crown that Mr. Moody is to wear because in all parts of the world, he has pointed people to the crucified One. It is the crown that faithful Sunday school teachers and devoted Christian workers are to wear.

I had in my home at one time a very celebrated Sunday school worker. He told me how he became a servant of Christ. He was converted as a boy before the Young People's Society of Christian Endeavor was known. He wanted to do something for Christ, and all he could think of was to teach a Sunday school class. He went to the superintendent with a request that he might be made a teacher, and was refused. He went a second time, with a similar result. He went a third time, and offered to bring in a class from outside, and this time he secured the consent of the superintendent. When he went out to find boys, his first visit was to a great brownstone mansion. He rang the bell, and the servant opened the door. He asked if he could speak to the lady of the house. He was shown into the parlor, and soon the mother of the boy entered.

He said, "I have come to ask if your boy can come to Sunday school."

Her face flushed and her eyes flashed as she replied, "My child has been to Sunday school before, and he has had such miserable teaching that I have made up my mind that he will not go again until either I can teach him myself or get someone who can."

After a little waiting, she asked, "Suppose I should send him; who would teach him?"

He became greatly embarrassed at this question, and he thought that if he ever got out of the house, he would never again think of doing any work in the church. Finally he replied, "Well, if he comes, I will teach him myself."

There was something in his direct statement – the ring of his voice – that touched the mother, and she said, "Next Sunday, he will be there."

He came. He was the only boy in the class, but when the young teacher told him the story of Jesus Christ, he was converted.

As he told us the story, there were tears in his eyes. He said, "Let me tell you the rest. Just before I left New York, I was called to the room of a man who was dying. As I entered, he called me to his bedside, and said, 'Come as close as you can.' I took his head and rested it on my arms, and we talked. He said, 'Teacher, has this not been a wonderful work?' His voice was almost gone, but he still whispered.

"Finally, his wife jumped up and cried, 'He is dying.' I held him closer and kissed him, for I loved him as though he had been my own child."

I will never forget how he looked as he added, "That was the boy I led to Christ. He was my associate in Sunday school work. We led hundreds of souls to Christ." Then with great emphasis, and in tears, he said, "I would rather have had the satisfaction of leading that one boy to Christ than to have conquered the whole world."

Such a work as this is possible to all people everywhere, and he who is thus faithful has a crown of rejoicing waiting for him. The hymn "Must I Go, and Empty-Handed?" was written by Charles Carroll Luther, who had heard a minister tell of a young man about thirty years old who was dying, and did not have one single soul to his credit. When the shadow of death fell across his face, someone near his bedside expressed concern for his happiness or his fear of death. He quickly answered, "I am not afraid to die. Jesus saves me now; but must I go, and empty-handed?"

Sadly, many of us may stand in the presence of the Master and be crownless in this respect.

The crown of glory. The fourth crown is the crown of glory. *And when the Chief Shepherd appears, you will receive the unfading crown of glory* (1 Peter 5:4). Peter seems to have a special message here for officers of the church, Sunday school teachers, and church members in general, for in fact, all of us are shepherds.

A shepherd is one who looks after the sheep, and the sheep that requires most of his attention is the one most likely to wander and fall by the wayside. We have a way of looking at the people, especially those who are newborn babes in Christ, and saying, "We will see how they hold out." If they stumble, we frequently exclaim, "It is just as I expected." That is a most unChristlike way to talk, and one that most deserves the censure of God!

God has placed before us the privilege of helping to support the weak ones in Christ.

The fact is that we are called into the church to be laborers together with God, and He has placed before us the privilege of helping to support the weak ones in Christ. There is not a time when one needs a warm handshake or a word of sympathy as much as when one is beginning his Christian life, just taking his first steps toward God. When my little girl first began to walk, she started to fall after she had taken one step, and I had to put my arms around her and hold her up. She walked in this way for days, but now we never think of holding her up. She can run along for the entire day and not be weary. To all those who are faithful in this special ministry, God has promised a sure reward.

The crown of righteousness. The fifth crown, and the last, seems to me the very best. It is the crown of righteousness. *In the future there is laid up for me the crown of righteousness, which the Lord, the righteous Judge, will award to me on that day; and not only to me, but also to all who have loved His appearing* (2 Timothy 4:8).

I have never yet been able to figure out just when the Lord will come again, for the Bible contains no such record, but with all my heart I am looking for Him. I do not know that He might not come today. He may come tomorrow. I am perfectly sure that the greatest blessing that could ever come to this world would be the visible presence of the Lord Himself. He would lift up the downtrodden. He Himself would relieve the oppressed, and He would apply the whip to the oppressor.

> It may be at morn, when the day is awaking,
>> When sunlight through darkness and shadow is
>> breaking,
> That Jesus will come in the fulness of glory,
>> To receive from the world "His own."
>
> Oh, joy! Oh, delight! Should we go without dying,
>> No sickness, no sadness, no dread, and no crying,
> Caught up through the clouds with our Lord into glory,
>> When Jesus receives "His own."[1]

---

1 These stanzas were written by H. L. Turner and are from the hymn that begins with "It may be morn, when the day is awaking."

This is how I am looking for Him, and I am longing for Him, and with all my soul I love His appearing; and unto every such person waiting, there is a crown promised.

> So I am watching and waiting
>   each moment of the day,
> If it be morn or evening
>   when He calleth me away;
>
> And it makes the day grow brighter,
>   and its trials easier borne,
> When I am saying every moment,
>   "Today the Lord may come."[2]

But there is something better still, and that is the full reward described in Revelation 4. This is a picture of the glorified church. We are told that the twenty-four elders came in with crowns upon their heads, clothed with white raiment, seated around the throne. Suddenly the King of Kings appears. At once the four and twenty elders fall down before Him, take off their crowns, and cast them before the throne, saying, *Worthy are You, our Lord and our God, to receive glory and honor and power* (Revelation 4:11). The best reward of all, then, is to be with Him.

That was a glad day in England in 1855 when the soldiers came back from the Crimean War, and the queen gave them medals, called Crimean medals. Galleries

---

2   This stanza seems to come from a hymn with an unknown author. The hymn begins with "When purple twilight gathers."

were constructed for the two Houses of Parliament and the royal family to witness the presentation. Her Majesty herself came in to give the soldiers their rewards. Here comes a colonel who lost both his feet at Inkerman; he is wheeled in on a chair. Here is a man whose arms are gone. And so they came, maimed and lame. Then the queen, in the name of the English people, gave the medals, and the thousands of people, with streaming eyes, sang "God Save the Queen."

However, I can think of something that would have made the scene more wonderful – if these men had taken off the medals that the queen had placed upon them, and cast them back at her feet, saying, "No, Your Majesty, we cannot keep them. We give back the medals. To see you is the greatest reward." That is what we will do in heaven.

I have a friend who was in the Crimean War. He told me that he had received that day a medal with "Inkerman" upon it, for that was his battle, but he said the most touching part of it all was the experience of a friend of his who had fought by his side. A cannon ball took off one of his legs, but the brave fellow sprang up immediately. He took hold of a tree, drew his sword, and was ready to fight even to death. Immediately another cannon ball came crashing past and took off his other leg. They carried him wounded, bleeding, and (as they supposed) dying to the hospital. Strangely enough, he came back to life again.

When the day came to award the medals, they carried him upon his stretcher before Her Majesty, the queen. She had simply given the medals by the hands of her secretary to the other soldiers, but when she saw this man carried in on a stretcher, with his face so thin and pale, she rose from her seat, bent down by his side, and pinned the medal upon his chest with her own hands while tears fell like rain upon the face of the brave soldier.

To see God in all His beauty will be the full reward.

This is how I trust it will be with many of us. We will come into His presence and stand face to face with Him. He will rise from His throne and come forward to receive us. As we look up into His face, thrones will vanish away and crowns will be as nothing, for to see Him in all His beauty will be the full reward.

Chapter 3

Rules for Service

No soldier in active service entangles himself in the affairs of everyday life, so that he may please the one who enlisted him as a soldier. Also if anyone competes as an athlete, he does not win the prize unless he competes according to the rules. – 2 Timothy 2:4-5

It is not enough to simply perform what might be called good deeds in the estimation of the world, for one might receive the applause of men and miss his reward at the hands of God. Neither is it enough for someone to be so given to service that he might win the applause of people everywhere. There is no special promise in God's Word written for the person who is simply faithful in outward service. Paul must have had this in mind when he said, *He does not win the prize unless he competes according to the rules.* It is a good thing for the Christian to compare his life, both public and private, his innermost thoughts and the hidden man of his heart, to the Word of God to see if in any point he is falling away from God's plan and the Holy Spirit's guidance.

Solemn Topic

When John, in Revelation 3:11, wrote, *Hold fast what you have, so that no one will take your crown*, he presented what to my mind is one of the most solemn topics in all the Bible – namely, that one might be saved, have his sins forgiven, stand before God justified, be perfectly sure of being ultimately received into His presence, and be saved throughout eternity, yet miss his reward and lose his crown.

This chapter is a note of warning and a heart cry to people everywhere to search their lives, aided by the Spirit, and to ask God to deal very thoroughly with them, even though this dealing may mean cutting off some sin that is very much loved or giving up some long-cherished plan.

All service must be prompted by right motives.

It is not so much how the work appears outwardly that commends it to God, for in this, His judgment is given differently from that of man. Instead, it is entirely a question as to what is behind it all that prompted the service. The giving of the widow's mite and its whole-hearted acceptance by our Master is an illustration of this fact, for in the desire that prompted the gift was found that which was of ten thousand times more value than the gift itself.

One might preach the gospel and win hundreds of souls for Christ, while the motives that prompted the preaching might have been wrong. One might oversee a Sunday school with much success, be a teacher of acknowledged ability, lead the young people's work in the church, and be a chosen leader of the mission work. In all these endeavors, he might have the seal of the

> The desire that prompted the gift was found that which was of ten thousand times more value than the gift itself.

approval of men and the praise of the multitude because of acknowledged success, yet miserably fail at the great day of awards to receive one single crown for faithfulness – simply because the work was born in selfishness and carried on in pride. It was not done for the glory of God, but rather for the glory of man.

One might build churches, and for his supposed generosity be highly esteemed by people, yet receive a rebuke from the lips of the risen Christ. One might endow schools that God would use for the betterment

27

of society and for the accomplishment of His own purposes or the working of His own plans, yet have no recognition on the great day of awards. One might give his money to clothe the poor and feed the hungry, or he might be known wherever the English language is spoken for his charitable works – yet when the great day of awards comes, he might hear the Master say, *I never knew you; depart from Me* (Matthew 7:23).

His soul is saved, but his life is lost. All of these things are true because, while outwardly the service was wonderful and the success great, the motive that prompted it all was selfish. Jesus Himself has said that there would be some who would say, *Lord, Lord, did we not prophesy in Your name, and in Your name cast out demons, and in Your name perform many miracles?* (Matthew 7:22). Thus the teaching becomes more intense and the lesson more startling, for one might even think that he is shaping his life according to God's plan, yet most terribly miss the reward.

When Paul wrote his first letter to the Corinthians, he said, *No man can lay a foundation other than the one which is laid, which is Jesus Christ. . . . If any man's work is burned up, he will suffer loss; but he himself will be saved, yet so as through fire* (1 Corinthians 3:11, 15). To my mind, this is very clearly a lesson to Christian workers in general, and to ministers in particular. The foundation is the same for us all – Jesus Christ – but the superstructure may be very different.

It is a most solemn thought, one of the most solemn I know, that when the great day of fire will come, each person's work will be tried according to what kind it is. The ministry of the man whom the world honored will be touched by fire. The service of the Christian worker, from the first effort made for Christ to the last, will certainly be tested. The teaching of the Sunday school teacher, throughout his or her entire Christian experience, will be brought beneath the searching light of the Son of God. The testimony of every Christian in every land will be searched through and through. The life in the home, in the place of business, in the streets, at home or in foreign lands, by day and by night, will be tested by the fire of God. If the work is burned, the person *will suffer loss; but he himself will be saved, yet so as through fire.* It is a tremendously solemn message.

> When the great day of fire will come, each person's work will be tried according to what kind it is.

I might have all the experience God has given me as a preacher, teacher, evangelist, father, husband, and friend, and then eventually stand before God with all my work swept away, going into His presence with the smell of fire upon my garments. God forbid! Paul had this fate in mind when he said, *Everyone who competes in the games exercises self-control in all things. They then do it to receive a perishable wreath, but we an imperishable. . . . But I discipline my body and make it my slave, so that, after I have preached to others, I myself will not be disqualified*, or (as we have already seen) "be disapproved" (1 Corinthians 9:25, 27).

May God keep us from meeting such an experience as this on that great day!

We must labor with clean hands.

God never uses an unclean person. It is possible that one may be saved, yet allow sin to control him in some way; but it is not possible for God to use that which is either common or unclean. *Depart, depart, go out from there, touch nothing unclean* (Isaiah 52:11; 2 Corinthians 6:17). From this command of Scripture, we learn that if one is in the very slightest touch with the world, he is against God, and he soon loses his power. He loses his testimony, and God sets him aside. *Search me, O God, and know my heart; try me and know my anxious thoughts; and see if there be any hurtful way in me* (Psalm 139:23-24) should be the cry of every Christian everywhere.

The old law touching the priesthood is a good thing for us to remember:

> *Then the* Lord *spoke to Moses, saying, "Tell Aaron and his sons to be careful with the holy gifts of the sons of Israel, which they dedicate to Me, so as not to profane My holy name; I am the* Lord. *Say to them, 'If any man among all your descendants through-out your generations approaches the holy gifts which the sons of Israel dedicate to the* Lord, *while he has an uncleanness, that person shall be cut off from before Me; I am the* Lord. (Leviticus 22:1-3)

The doctrine of separation in the Old Testament for the priests is for us in the New Testament, for Peter tells us that all believers are priests unto God. The Old Testament doctrine has, however, been intensified by the teaching and the touch of Jesus Christ.

You shall set the turban on his head and put the holy crown on the turban. Then you shall take the anointing oil and pour it on his head and anoint him (Exodus 29:6-7). The anointing oil put upon the head of the priest was a sign that he was separated from all worldly services and every selfish principle of life. From that moment on, he was not his own man, but God's. The oil in the Old Testament represents the Holy Spirit in the New Testament, and whether we have recognized it or not, it is nevertheless true. By the Spirit of God we have been regenerated, by that same Spirit we have been made alive, and by the same Spirit we have been sealed or anointed as God's own special treasure. If we have not allowed Him to use us, we have robbed Him of His right, and at the great day of awards, we will be called to a strict account.

> If we have not allowed God to use us, we have robbed Him of His right.

> *The priest who is the highest among his brothers, on whose head the anointing oil has been poured and who has been consecrated to wear the garments, shall not uncover his head nor tear his clothes; nor shall he approach any dead person, nor defile himself even for his father or his*

> *mother; nor shall he go out of the sanc-*
> *tuary nor profane the sanctuary of his*
> *God, for the consecration of the anointing*
> *oil of his God is on him; I am the* LORD.
> (Leviticus 21:10-12)

How close this teaching is, and how completely many of us are condemned by it as we apply it to our own lives!

Yet there is no reason for discouragement. In the olden times, when the priests or the people were in touch with sin, the ashes of the red heifer were sprinkled upon them for cleansing, and immediately they stepped back into fellowship and God clothed them with power. In the New Testament, a better provision is made:

> *For if the blood of goats and bulls and the*
> *ashes of a heifer sprinkling those who have*
> *been defiled sanctify for the cleansing of*
> *the flesh, how much more will the blood*
> *of Christ, who through the eternal Spirit*
> *offered Himself without blemish to God,*
> *cleanse your conscience from dead works to*
> *serve the living God?* (Hebrews 9:13-14)

I have not been able to find in the New Testament, with the exception of the Lord's Prayer, any place where it is said that the Christian must ask for forgiveness of sins; but I do read in 1 John 1:7-9:

> *If we walk in the Light as He Himself is*
> *in the Light, we have fellowship with one*

another, and the blood of Jesus His Son
cleanses us from all sin. If we say that we
have no sin, we are deceiving ourselves
and the truth is not in us. If we confess our
sins, He is faithful and righteous to for-
give us our sins and to cleanse us from all
unrighteousness.

I learn then that if I confess my sins, He is faithful and just to forgive them and to cleanse me perfectly; and when He forgives sin, He always forgets it.

Chapter 4

A Note of Warning

It is to the praise of God that He has in His Word given us repeated instances of people who have fallen so that they might serve as a warning. Their very failure should be an inspiration to us to avoid similar mistakes. One cannot read the story of Adam and Eve without getting a glimpse both of the power of Satan in his overthrow of our first parents and the tenderness of God as He cried out in the cool of the day, *Where are you?* (Genesis 3:9). We cannot study the life and character of Noah without being affected by the fact that someone might be used of God today, then tomorrow wander so far away from Him as to make serious mistakes. All of the Old Testament is a cry for those who have wandered away from God to return. In their wanderings, we get our lessons; and in God's cry, we have certain evidence that although we may have sinned, yet He is always ready to put our sins away from Him and from us.

One of the best illustrations in the Old Testament, to my mind, is that of Saul. He made a splendid appearance as a king. When the people demanded a king, God sent Samuel to seek one out, and he found Saul, whose appearance was kingly. If nothing else recommended him to the throne, this did. The first thing Samuel did was to pour the anointing oil upon his head, which was an indication that God was taking him for His own, thus separating him from the world. A little later we read that the Spirit of the Lord came upon Saul, and it looks as if he must have been filled with His presence and must have fulfilled the highest expectations of the people. A little farther on in his history, the man of God appeared to him, saying, *The Lord is with you, O valiant warrior.*[3]

> God is always ready to put our sins away from Him and from us.

As we look upon him, we have come to the conclusion that it is indeed true. When the people cry out for the king, and Saul is called forth, he stands head and shoulders above the people gathered around him, and involuntarily the people, when they looked upon him, were stirred to such enthusiasm that they shouted, *Long live the king* (1 Samuel 10:23-24).

---

3   This was said to Gideon (Judges 6:12).

Afterward, when Saul went to Gibeah, *the valiant men whose hearts God had touched went with him* (1 Samuel 10:26). Thus the story goes on, with Saul rising ever higher and higher in the popular esteem and favor. Yet in the end, and in the face of it all, he darkened the pages of the Old Testament, made the ruling of his kingdom a failure, and died by his own hand (which really, in the sight of God, makes him a murderer).

One cannot read such a story as this without trembling, and it is for each one of us today that the Bible was written so that we might know God and that we might know ourselves.

I have learned from this story of Saul, the king, that it is possible for someone to be born of the Spirit, really to be saved, and to be saved forever, yet miserably fail in the sight of God.

I remember preaching in one of the cities of Indiana. For four days, the church was crowded, but a crowd is not an indication of a blessing. Not infrequently, the presence of a crowd is an indication of defeat, for preachers are inclined under such circumstances to put their confidence in people rather than in God. During all four days, not a hand was lifted for prayer, nor a single indication given that there might be an awakening on the part of the Christian people.

The field I was to labor in next seemed quite ready for the harvest, and in the preparatory services, many people were saved. I called the ministers of the Indiana city together and asked them to give me the privilege of closing my engagement with them, telling them that there was some barrier in the way of the working of God's Spirit, and that I felt when I preached as if I was bound with chains. After a little conference, one of the ministers requested that the decision be withheld for a little while, stating that he felt sure that he knew where the difficulty was. We had one of the members of this minister's church as the leader of our force of personal workers. He was a man well known throughout his own state, and he was a judge of one of the highest courts. Somehow, though, it seemed that when this man passed through the audience, he sent a cold wave over the people.

The pastor of this church left this conference of ministers and went into the office of this old judge and said to him, "I have been hearing rumors on the streets for a long time that your life is not clean, and I have come to say that if these rumors are untrue, I desire to take some public stand with you to contradict them; but I have also come to say that if they are true, I will stand nearer to you than a brother and will help you get free from the power of your besetting sin."

The old judge looked a moment at him, and then put his head on his arms on the desk and sobbed out, "They are all true, and more."

In a moment, they were on their knees in prayer, and it was only a moment more before the old judge rose as a delivered man, free from the power of his sin.

I was just lifting my hands to pronounce the benediction at the close of an afternoon service when the church door opened and the old judge came in. Having lifted his hand to ask permission to speak, he made this statement: "My friends, I have been known for years as one of the members of the church and as an officer of the church, but for a long time, my life has been robbed of its power and my soul of its peace. I have lost my influence in my home, and I fear that I have almost completely lost my influence in my city. But I have gotten right with my minister and right with God, and I have come to ask your forgiveness."

The confession was made with sobs. There was no benediction pronounced that afternoon. The people all filed out one way. Some took the hand of the judge to say, "God bless you," and some came to say nothing, but to pass by with burning hearts and cheeks wet with tears. When the evening service came and the sermon had been preached, there was a remarkable change. The atmosphere seemed like heaven. At least fifty people pressed their way to the front to accept Christ as their Savior. The first man to come was the old judge, with his arm around a poor lost man who was soon hopefully saved. In less than six days, more than five hundred people came pressing their way into the kingdom of God.

> We can only be kept full by living in close fellowship with the Lord Jesus Christ.

It is likewise a possible thing to have been filled with the Spirit at one time, and then to make a failure of one's life. It is not enough to live on the old experiences, no matter how precious they may have been. It is not enough to have been filled once, but we must be kept full all the time, and we can only be kept full by living in close fellowship and uninterrupted communion with the Lord Jesus Christ.

I wholeheartedly agree with F. B. Meyer's interpretation of the expression, *I myself will not be disqualified*, or a castaway. Certainly we know men today who were once used of God in preaching and blessed by Him in soul winning, but who are set aside today. In other words, they have become castaways. They are objects of pity, both to angels and to men. Mr. Meyer, in describing these people, tells us of his stylographic pen. It was one of some value, and it had been given to him for his private use. For a long time, he carried it with him everywhere and used it on all occasions. Then a more improved version came out, and he used the new one instead of the old. The old one was still his, but it was disapproved and set aside.

Mr. Meyer says he can imagine what the pen would say as it thought of the past: "There was once a time when he used me always – and now, never. There was a time when I knew his thoughts before anyone else, and now I am set aside. There was a time when I was his closest companion, and now I am never used."

Sadly, many men who have preached the gospel with power in days gone by, whom God has delighted to use, could say the same thing. This book is sent forth as a warning so that all such men might turn right around now. Let no man at the end take your crown.

Why Saul Fell

There were several reasons why Saul fell. In the first place, he was jealous of David. It awakened all the hatred in his soul to see David beloved and honored while these things had been denied to him. But that is not the end of his sin. It really seems as if jealousy must have been born in hell. If one has the seed of jealousy in his nature, he is somehow compelled by a force he can hardly resist to go deeper into the evil.

In the second place, we find Saul destroying the Lord's truest friend. How true it is that when we have committed one sin and fail to make that one right, the rest becomes easy, and frequently almost a delight.

In the third place, we find him sparing Agag and the part of his flock. He, the king, with lying upon his lips! This sin becomes very easy. If we allow the corruption of two or three days to lie in our souls without being cleansed, how sad the results! No one should close his eyes at night until he has absolutely made certain that all of the sins of the day have been washed away in the precious blood of Christ.

The last we see of Saul is when he falls upon his sword and takes his own life, making him a murderer in the sight of God and in the sight of man.

Sin is awful. In the very beginning of it, you seem to get the hiss of the serpent as he trails through the garden of Eden. It breaks up homes and drags multitudes away from God and down to hell. The warning cry is given here that we must forsake the small sins if we do not want

> We must forsake the small sins if we do not want to be overpowered by the greater ones.

to be overpowered by the greater ones. We must be cleansed from little transgressions if we do not want to finally be lost. If anyone would ask the secret of failure, the reason why the crown would be lost in the end, the answer could be summed up in three letters: S-I-N.

Chapter 5

Then Comes the End

Then comes the end. – 1 Corinthians 15:24

The day of awards is a great day. It is really the judgment seat of Christ, when we are to receive the reward of the deeds done through the body (2 Corinthians 5:10). It is not a time when we are judged for sin, for the sin question was settled at the cross for those who accept Jesus Christ. It is not identical with the great white throne judgment presented in Revelation 20. It is simply the day when the Master, before whom the records of our lives are laid bare, will give to us the reward for our faithfulness or express His assessment of our faithlessness.

I can see the Master with His people gathered before Him. A name is called that is familiar, and I see that person standing before Him with great expectancy. Then the Master speaks with that voice that John tells us is *like the sound of many waters* (Revelation 14:2), that voice that stilled the tempest-tossed sea (Matthew 8:26) and caused Lazarus to break the bands of death (John 11:43-44).

I hear Him speak. The crowns are being lifted up, and the first one is the crown of life. I hear Him say, "This is given to the one who has done little things well for My glory, or to the one who has suffered for My sake. You could have had it, but you failed in your own home. You had no testimony for your own circle of friends. You could have spoken a kind word, but you left it unsaid. The cup of cold water was never given. You could have had the crown of life, but another has taken it."

I see Him hold up the second crown. He says, "This is given to the one who has done difficult work for Me. I suffered the pains of Gethsemane, the ridicule of the crowd, the stripes of the Roman scourger, and the pains of hell upon the cross. This crown is for the one who has endured all things so that My cause could be advanced. But then, when there came a time when the church seemed about to move forward, you opposed it. When thousands of souls might have been converted, your prejudice against the work of the Holy Spirit blocked the blessing. You could have had the crown, but another has taken it."

I see Him lift high the third crown, brilliant with jewels. All the angels shout aloud, "This is the soul winner's crown." There has always been joy in the presence of the angels of God over those redeemed from sin (Luke 15:10). Jesus declares, "You could have had this crown, but sadly, your culture, your intellectual strength, and your social position never won a soul for Me. The members of your own household were led into My kingdom by others. The people in your own business did not know you were Mine."

I remember once holding a series of meetings in Paris, Illinois. As I was walking down the street with one of my assistants, I heard him talking with a young man, asking him to be a Christian, but making no impression upon him. I heard him say, "Your mother wants you to become a Christian, does she not?" The young man began to cry. Then I heard him ask, "Your father wants you to become a Christian, does he not?" There was no answer.

Soon, though, I heard him make this statement: "My father is an officer in the church, and my mother is a leader in the work of the women's society in the church, but neither of them has ever spoken to me about my soul."

I believe many fathers and mothers will stand before the Judge on the great day of awards and hear the words, "You are crownless. Your children were not saved, or if they were, you have had no part in their salvation. You could have had this crown, but another has taken it."

I can see Him holding high the fourth crown, the crown of glory. I can hear Him describe how one person came into the church from great depths of sin; how his character had been undermined by the power of an evil life; how he had been saved by the power of God and encouraged by a warm handshake and a sympathizing word, and a brother's compassion to urge him to hold out to the end. And I can almost hear Him say, "Such a person sat beside you in church and walked with you on the streets, or in the store, or possibly lived with you in your home – and you never said a word. You let him slip away from fellowship with Christ, and when he wandered, you exclaimed in surprise, 'That is what I expected from him.'"

I can catch the tone of His voice as He says, "You could have had this crown, but another has taken it."

I see Him hold up the fifth and last crown, the crown of righteousness. I hear Him say, "Did not I promise that I would come again? Had not I written it over and over again in the Book? Was not line added to line and statement added to statement that in the same manner as I went away, I would come back? Were not all the prophecies of My coming fulfilled, even to the last details of My life, My suffering, and My death? Did you not have faith that if one prophecy was fulfilled, the others would have been fulfilled also?"

And then that crown, which to me is the most beautiful, the brightest and the best, is held aloft for a moment, dazzling in its glory, and I hear Him say, "You could have had this crown, but another has taken it."

We may miss the five crowns by our unfaithfulness, yet we may be saved, *so as through fire* (1 Corinthians 3:15). But one thing must be: we must see Him face to face.

In the city of Indianapolis, a well-known Quaker minister told me about a friend whose child had been born blind. He was brought to Indianapolis, and this Quaker was asked to find a specialist who would successfully treat him. Such a person was found. When the operation had been finished, he announced that the boy would certainly see. Sure enough, he opened his eyes. His first glance rested upon his mother, whom he had never known except by finger touch. The mother bent down to see if her son would recognize her. She cried out, "Oh, my son! My son!"

The boy gazed at his mother, and when he recognized her, he exclaimed, "Oh, Mother, is this heaven?"

It will be heaven for us when the scales are taken from our eyes, the veil that dims our vision is removed, and we see Him face to face. We may miss every crown mentioned in the New Testament, but we cannot fail to see Him. I do not know if there can be sadness in heaven, but what feeling will it be that will take possession of us when we hear Him say, "You could have had the crown, but another has taken it"?

> We may miss every crown mentioned in the New Testament, but we cannot fail to see God.

What feeling will it be that will possess us when we hear Him say, *Well done, good and faithful [servant.] . . . Enter into the joy of your master* (Matthew 25:23), and we will have the five crowns and a glimpse of His face!

Chapter 6:

The Holy Spirit in His Relation to the Church

*And the Lord was adding to their number
day by day those who were being saved.*
– Acts 2:47

In the honest endeavor that we properly make to live
the Christian life, and in the end receive a reward from
the hand of the Master, thereby not missing our crown,
the Holy Spirit is our helper more than all others. He is
certainly to be considered to be the director and leader
of our church life. We do not need to expect any great

outpouring of the Holy Spirit as long as His leadership is ignored, and without this high spiritual atmosphere, we may expect, as individuals, no special victories.

On the day of Pentecost, two great events occurred. The first was the exaltation of Jesus Christ at the right hand of the Father. *This Jesus God raised up again, to which we are all witnesses* (Acts 2:32). The other was the outpouring of the Spirit because Jesus had been raised up and exalted. The point is that Christ as our head had the Holy Spirit poured out upon Him, thus receiving Him in trust for the body. It naturally follows that what the head has received, the members of the body have a right to claim.

Since that day, in the plan of God, the Holy Spirit has been the administrator of the affairs of the church, and He is here to make Christ real to every believer. If Jesus had tarried with us in the flesh and I had claimed His presence, He would have been denied to you; but now that He is present in the Spirit, we may all have Him and lay claim to His presence, and the love of God may be shed abroad in our hearts by the Holy Spirit (Romans 5:5). He is in a real sense the representative of Christ, and there can be no other. The Son of God is today at the right hand of God, representing the church, and the Spirit of God should be enthroned and exalted in the church, representing the risen Christ. He is to counsel her, guide her, and control her. Basically, He is to govern all things in the church, from the smallest things to the greatest.

The Scriptures are evidence that He has a message for the church. It is generally believed that the epistles to the seven churches in the book of Revelation contain the prophetic setting forth of the church's history, including its declines and recoveries, its failures and returns. It is believed by many that we have come to the Laodicean period of history of the last days of the church. Seven times we have the expression repeated: *He who has an ear, let him hear what the Spirit says to the churches* (e.g., Revelation 2:29).

It is to be noted that this expression is used after each of the churches had backslidden. Ephesus had left her first love. Smyrna was rich, and likely to be proud. Pergamos was touched with the doctrine of Balaam. Thyatira was influenced by Jezebel. Sardis had a name to live, and was dead. Philadelphia had but little strength. Laodicea was neither hot nor cold. The real cure for backsliding in the church is that which comes to us by the Holy Spirit of the revelation of God's will and the interpretation of God's Word.

> The real cure for backsliding in the church is that which comes to us by the Holy Spirit of the revelation of God's will

The church is a called-out body. We were chosen in Him before the world's foundation (Ephesians 1:4), and we are elect according to the foreknowledge of God (1 Peter 1:2), for that is what the Bible says. Jesus is in heaven directing the work of the church, but the Holy Spirit is here carrying out the plan. This plan extends to the smallest details of the life of the church. He has ordained the offices we must have and the kind of men we must lay hold upon to fill them. *Therefore* *it says, "When He ascended on high, He led captive a host of captives, and He gave gifts to men. . . . And He gave some as apostles, and some as prophets, and some as evangelists, and some as pastors and teachers, for the equipping of the saints for the work of service, to the building up of the body of Christ* (Ephesians 4:8, 11-12).

The church is really the habitation of God. Hear what the Scriptures have to say:

> *So then you are no longer strangers and aliens, but you are fellow citizens with the saints, and are of God's household, having been built on the foundation of the apostles and prophets, Christ Jesus Himself being the corner stone, in whom the whole building, being fitted together, is growing into a holy temple in the Lord, in whom you also are being built together into a dwelling of God in the Spirit.* (Ephesians 2:19-22)

If He is dwelling in us, we must be careful of our church life, for we may both grieve Him and quench Him by the way we live and work. Many things are done today in the church that may commend themselves to men, yet fall entirely short of the approval of God. As an illustration, Peter, standing up with the one hundred and twenty, spoke of the departure of Judas and declared that someone must be chosen in his place. Prayer was offered, a vote was taken, and Matthias was elected (Acts 1:15-26). However, there was no indication that this election was ever approved by the Lord, for Matthias at once sinks out of sight. Two years later, the Lord called Saul of Tarsus to fill the vacancy. Paul said this about himself: *Paul, an apostle (not sent from men nor through the agency of man, but through Jesus Christ and God the Father, who raised Him from the dead)* (Galatians 1:1).

The church was established by signs and wonders.

> *When the day of Pentecost had come, they were all together in one place. And suddenly there came from heaven a noise like a violent rushing wind, and it filled the whole house where they were sitting. And there appeared to them tongues as of fire distributing themselves, and they rested on each one of them. And they were all filled with the Holy Spirit and began to speak with other tongues, as the Spirit was giving them utterance.* (Acts 2:1-4)

> *God also testifying with them, both by signs and wonders and by various miracles and by gifts of the Holy Spirit according to His own will* (Hebrews 2:4).

There was no church in the Old Testament. This is the opinion of many Bible teachers. In Acts 2:41 we read, *So then, those who had received his word were baptized; and that day there were added about three thousand souls.* Some versions have "added *unto them*," and the "unto them" is written in italics, so that the original is *there were added about three thousand souls.* But we must add to something when we add, so in Acts 2:47 we read, *And the Lord was adding [to the church,* or *to their number] day by day those who were being saved.* But there is a still better explanation. In Acts 5:14 we read that they were *added to their number,* or even better, *added to the Lord.*

This is Paul's understanding of the church. Christ is the head, and the church is His body. We are being called out now from the gentile world. Every new soul won for Christ comes in to complete the body. Someday the last person will come in, and the skies will brighten with the return of the Lord.

It is this that gives one the passion for soul winning. It is this thought that furnishes the inspiration for the foreign missionary. The church is a called-out body, and the missionary is sent to Africa, to China, to Japan, and all around the world so that he may work in the fellowship of the Holy Spirit in leading souls to Christ. May God quickly bring the day when the last member of the body will be found!

The church is enlightened by the Spirit. The Spirit is the breath of God in the body of His church. If His rule is not followed, it naturally results that His life is shut out. It is like a man suffering from pneumonia. Someone who is unaccustomed to such scenes declares that the man needs more air, but the truth is that he does not need more air at all, but he needs more of his lungs to be filled with air. We do not need more of the

Holy Spirit, but the Holy Spirit should have more of the church. Sometimes, because His rule is not followed, He somewhat withdraws Himself and allows the forms to stay – but the power is departed. The oil is gone, but the lamp is there. There are churches where prayer is offered, the Bible is read, and people religiously attend church, and there is positively not even the resemblance of power. They are described in the words of Scripture as *that you have a name that you are alive, but you are dead* (Revelation 3:1). They remind us of the guard found in the excavated city of Pompeii. He stood with his helmet and his armor on, and his bony finger clasping his spear, yet not living. It is just the same with the church.

> We do not need more of the Holy Spirit, but the Holy Spirit should have more of the church.

A little thing at first may result in loss of power in the entire church. A wrong financial policy might do it. A spirit of criticism might accomplish it.

> There is an insidious disease which slowly and secretly turns the vital organs of the body to bone. It begins by ossifying little fragments of tissue here and there. No medical skill can arrest its progress. Nature is perverted from her healthy process of assimilating and nutrition, to the creation in the system of nothing but bone. What should be life to muscle and nerve and sinew and arteries turns to solid and lifeless bone. At length the heart is reached, and

vital parts of it become bone, and its beautiful work of pulsation, by which life is sent in red streams to the very tips of the fingers, ceases, and death ensues. Such is the moral induration which the sensibilities of a soul suffer, when long appealed to by the services of religion, to which it will not give back a throb of responsive feeling.[4]

If the church is to be governed by the Holy Spirit, every office bearer in the church should be influenced by the Holy Spirit. Ministers should be filled. Paul gives an illustration of one phase of this truth:

> *Saul, who was also known as Paul, filled with the Holy Spirit, fixed his gaze on him, and said, "You who are full of all deceit and fraud, you son of the devil, you enemy of all righteousness, will you not cease to make crooked the straight ways of the Lord? Now, behold, the hand of the Lord is upon you, and you will be blind and not see the sun for a time." And immediately a mist and a darkness fell upon him, and he went about seeking those who would lead him by the hand. Then the proconsul believed when he saw what had happened, being amazed at the teaching of the Lord.* (Acts 13:9-12)

---

4   This is a quote from the book *The Old Testament: A Living Book for All Ages* by Austin Phelps (1820-1890).

The Holy Spirit only fills the person whose desire is to honor Christ. Philosophy, poetry, art, sociology, and ethics are well enough in their places, but their place is not in the pulpit. The Holy Spirit has pledged Himself to witness only to the story of Jesus and the resurrection. Paul thought this whole thing out, and while he was educated in all the learning of the day, he said, *We preach Christ crucified, to Jews a stumbling block and to Gentiles foolishness, but to those who are the called, both Jews and Greeks, Christ the power of God and the wisdom of God* (1 Corinthians 1:23-24).

Peter is another illustration: *Then Peter, filled with the Holy Spirit, said to them, Rulers and elders of the people* (Acts 4:8). *As I began to speak, the Holy Spirit fell upon them just as He did upon us at the beginning. And I remembered the word of the Lord, how He used to say, "John baptized with water, but you will be baptized with the Holy Spirit"* (Acts 11:15-16).

I do not know of anyone in the New Testament Scripture furnishing us a better argument for the use of the Word of God in preaching than Peter himself. Take the sermon at Pentecost, if you will. It is simply a string of texts of Scripture. If you would ask, "But is this all he said?" I answer, "The words of Scripture are all that the Holy Spirit thought worthy to record." Peter's words would have passed away with his own generation. The Word of God abides forever.

Stephen provides an illustration of the fact that to be filled with the Holy Spirit does not always mean human success:

The statement found approval with the whole congregation; and they chose Stephen, a man full of faith and of the Holy Spirit, and Philip, Prochorus, Nicanor, Timon, Parmenas and Nicolas, a proselyte from Antioch. And these they brought before the apostles; and after praying, they laid their hands on them. The word of God kept on spreading; and the number of the disciples continued to increase greatly in Jerusalem, and a great many of the priests were becoming obedient to the faith. And Stephen, full of grace and power, was performing great wonders and signs among the people. . . . But being full of the Holy Spirit, he gazed intently into heaven and saw the glory of God, and Jesus standing at the right hand of God. (Acts 6:5-8; 7:55)

Someone might be filled with the Spirit and pass through the greatest disappointment of his life. Stephen was just as truly filled, although he was stoned to death, as Peter, the preacher of Pentecost, was. God might fill you and then test you. The great guns that are used in the defense of our country are always tested before they leave the arsenal.

> Someone might be filled with the Spirit and pass through the greatest disappointment of his life.

The position of the minister is an exalted one. *It was revealed to them that they were not serving themselves, but you, in these things which now have been announced to you through those who preached the gospel to you by the Holy Spirit sent from heaven—things into which angels long to look* (1 Peter 1:12).

There is not an angel in the skies today who would not leave his post of honor to take your place and mine in preaching the gospel. The position is a divine one: *Be on guard for yourselves and for all the flock, among which the Holy Spirit has made you overseers, to shepherd the church of God which He purchased with His own blood* (Acts 20:28). It greatly dignifies our work to know that we are here to do just what Jesus would do if He were in our place.

The message of the man of God is inspired: *For it is not you who speak, but it is the Spirit of your Father who speaks in you* (Matthew 10:20). *The gospel must first be preached to all the nations. When they arrest you and hand you over, do not worry beforehand about what you are to say, but say whatever is given you in that hour; for it is not you who speak, but it is the Holy Spirit* (Mark 13:10-11). *The Holy Spirit will teach you in that very hour what you ought to say* (Luke 12:12).

The Holy Spirit never encourages idleness. We are not teaching the lesson that one needs to simply open his mouth and expect the Lord to fill it, but the ideal position is for everyone to be so filled with the message all the time that if he were called to speak any number of times during the day, he would always be sure that he had a message from God. Notice what the Scriptures say: *I was in the Spirit on the Lord's day, and I heard behind me a loud voice like the sound of a trumpet* (Revelation 1:10). *Immediately I was in the Spirit; and*

behold, a throne was standing in heaven, and One sit-
ting on the throne (Revelation 4:2). If a man of God is
saturated with his message, and is in the Spirit, there
will be no question as to his power in the presentation
of what he has to say.

Once these conditions are fulfilled, the results are
guaranteed:

> *He said to them, "Go into all the world and*
> *preach the gospel to all creation. He who*
> *has believed and has been baptized shall*
> *be saved; but he who has disbelieved shall*
> *be condemned. These signs will accompany*
> *those who have believed: in My name they*
> *will cast out demons, they will speak with*
> *new tongues; they will pick up serpents, and*
> *if they drink any deadly poison, it will not*
> *hurt them; they will lay hands on the sick,*
> *and they will recover.* (Mark 16:15-18)

God also testifying with them, both by signs and wonders
and by various miracles and by gifts of the Holy Spirit
according to His own will (Hebrews 2:4). There is absolutely no limit to God's power; He can do all things.

There is a very significant expression used in
Revelation 14:13: *I heard a voice from heaven, saying,*
"Write, 'Blessed are the dead who die in the Lord from
now on!'" "Yes," says the Spirit, "so that they may rest
from their labors, for their deeds follow with them." F.
B. Meyer thinks that this *"Yes," says the Spirit* is to be
interpreted as *"Amen," says the Spirit,* and that it is the

Spirit's approval of what we have done in the name of Christ. It will be a glad day for the church when for every pastor's work, the Spirit will breathe "Amen"; when He will say "Amen" for the service of every elder, deacon, and trustee; and when all the living saints will live so nearly according to God's will that at the close of each day, the Spirit will say "Amen and amen."

However, the filling of the Holy Spirit is not to be confined to those who are called ministers of the gospel. Every deacon should be filled: *Therefore, brethren, select from among you seven men of good reputation, full of the Spirit and of wisdom, whom we may put in charge of this task. But we will devote ourselves to prayer and to the ministry of the word* (Acts 6:3-4).

> The filling of the Holy Spirit is not to be confined to those who are called ministers of the gospel.

There was a time in the history of the church when men were chosen to fill the church's offices, not because of their social position or their financial ability, but simply because they were men filled with the Holy Spirit. That is the only one real test of fitness for such an office. I feel very sure that we should expect a Pentecostal outpouring of the Spirit of God only when this principle is recognized.

If the Holy Spirit is the life of the church, then we are to be exceedingly careful with respect to everything that would grieve Him in the least. *Let all bitterness and wrath and anger and clamor and slander be put away from you, along with all malice. Be kind to one* *another, tender-hearted, forgiving each other, just as God in Christ also has forgiven you* (Ephesians 4:31-32). It is a new thought to some that the presence of bitterness or wrath or anger would grieve the Spirit, but this is indeed the case.

The Holy Spirit is to work out in us that which Christ has accomplished for us on the throne. There can only be one hindrance to the working out of this plan of God, and that is found in the church itself. There is a solemn warning for all the members of the church: *Do not quench the Spirit* (1 Thessalonians 5:19).

> But Peter said, "Ananias, why has Satan filled your heart to lie to the Holy Spirit and to keep back some of the price of the land? While it remained unsold, did it not remain your own? And after it was sold, was it not under your control? Why is it that you have conceived this deed in your heart? You have not lied to men but to God." And as he heard these words, Ananias fell down and breathed his last; and great fear came over all who heard of it. The young men got up and covered him up, and after carrying him out, they buried him.
>
> Now there elapsed an interval of about three hours, and his wife came in, not knowing what had happened. And Peter responded to her, "Tell me whether you sold the land for such and such a price?" And she

said, "Yes, that was the price." Then Peter said to her, "Why is it that you have agreed together to put the Spirit of the Lord to the test? Behold, the feet of those who have buried your husband are at the door, and they will carry you out as well. (Acts 5:3-9)

While people may not nowadays have been struck down as Ananias and Sapphira were, yet it is true that because of the fact that we are living in a spirit that is contrary to the Holy Spirit, we become dead spiritually, if not physically. It is possible to so nearly quench the Spirit that from the human standpoint, there will be no life at all.

It is possible to so nearly quench the Spirit that from the human standpoint, there will be no life at all.

Thus, while the individual member of the church may miss his reward and *be saved, yet so as through fire*, the same thing may be true of the church as a whole. It would be a sad thing for the Bridegroom to be disappointed in His bride.

Chapter 7

The Gospel in the Old Testament

*The birds of prey came down upon the
carcasses, and Abram drove them away.*
– Genesis 15:11

In all parts of the Word of God, both in the Old
Testament and the New, we find God's provision made
for cleansing the sinner. If, in the light of all that has been
said, we feel ourselves condemned, and that if the day of
awards came tomorrow we would suffer loss and lose our
crown, though we *will be saved, yet so as through fire*, the
thought should come to us as an inspiration that all our
sins may be blotted out and our transgressions forgiven.

It is of great encouragement, therefore, for us to study the subject now given. It is not necessary that we should simply familiarize ourselves with the New Testament. Of course, this is essential, but if we desire to know God's ability to cleanse, we should know the Old Testament Scriptures with their types and ceremonies.

The birds of the Bible form an interesting subject for investigation. The first mention of them in the Old Testament is in Genesis 1:21: *God created the great sea monsters and every living creature that moves, with which the waters swarmed after their kind, and every winged bird after its kind; and God saw that it was good.* Since that time, they can be seen flying through many of the stories of the Holy Bible, filled with lessons of sweetness and power. Their songs have been the sweetest, their feathers have been the brightest, and their teaching has been the best. The eagle mounting up far above the earth and building its nest above the clouds is a picture of Christian exhilaration. Isaiah had it in mind when he said,

> The eagle mounting up far above the earth is a picture of Christian exhilaration.

Those who wait for the LORD will gain new strength; they will mount up with wings like eagles, they will run and not get tired, they will walk and not become weary (Isaiah 40:31).

The same bird, preparing its nest and pushing out its little ones so that they may learn to fly, offers a splendid illustration of the providence of God, perhaps seeming a little harsh, but with the outcome always glorious. Everyone who has come to know God in Christ must certainly say with the apostle Paul that *God causes all things to work together for good to those who love God* (Romans 8:28). When Elijah was at the brook Cherith, and the waters had passed from his vision, and he himself was on the verge of starvation, the birds fed him (1 Kings 17:6). Every little sparrow that comes fluttering through the air is a reminder of what Jesus said, that even a sparrow does not fall to the ground without our heavenly Father knowing it (Matthew 10:29).

As we read the Old Testament stories, we find that there are also birds of prey. They, too, have their lessons, but the stories they tell are not so bright and happy. This lesson in the text is along this line.

Abram is a wonderful study for the Christian. In the great events of his life, he perfectly typifies the experience through which every Christian has passed. When God called him from Ur of the Chaldees, he was an illustration of our being called from the land of sin and death. By separating himself from Terah, his father-in-law, he emphasized what Jesus said, that we must forsake father and mother and our own life if we want to be His disciple (Luke 14:33). Every Christian, if he is to be used of God, must forsake the world. In Abram's separation from Lot, he is a perfect illustration of the demand made in the New Testament that we must, if we desire to be filled with the Holy Spirit of God, separate ourselves even from the flesh.

When we read the connection of the text with other verses of Scripture, we learn that there is a great battle waging. It is written in Genesis 14:14-16:

> *When Abram heard that his relative had*
> *been taken captive, he led out his trained*
> *men, born in his house, three hundred and*
> *eighteen, and went in pursuit as far as Dan.*
> *He divided his forces against them by night,*
> *he and his servants, and defeated them,*
> *and pursued them as far as Hobah, which*
> *is north of Damascus. He brought back all*
> *the goods, and also brought back his rela-*
> *tive Lot with his possessions, and also the*
> *women, and the people.*

We find here a real test of Abram. Many men have gone down just where Abram stood. God is always giving us tests of character.

Read Genesis 14:21-24 very carefully, and notice Abram's answer:

> *The king of Sodom said to Abram, "Give the*
> *people to me and take the goods for your-*
> *self." Abram said to the king of Sodom, "I*
> *have sworn to the LORD God Most High,*
> *possessor of heaven and earth, that I will*
> *not take a thread or a sandal thong or any-*
> *thing that is yours, for fear you would say, 'I*
> *have made Abram rich.' I will take noth-*
> *ing except what the young men have eaten,*
> *and the share of the men who went with*
> *me, Aner, Eshcol, and Mamre; let them take*
> *their share."*

It always pays to stand for God as opposed to people in this world. This is clearly taught in Genesis 15:1-10:

> After these things the word of the LORD came to Abram in a vision, saying, "Do not fear, Abram, I am a shield to you; your reward shall be very great." Abram said, "O Lord God, what will You give me, since I am childless, and the heir of my house is Eliezer of Damascus?" And Abram said, "Since You have given no offspring to me, one born in my house is my heir." Then behold, the word of the LORD came to him, saying, "This man will not be your heir; but one who will come forth from your own body, he shall be your heir." And He took him outside and said, "Now look toward the heavens, and count the stars, if you are able to count them." And He said to him, "So shall your descendants be." Then he believed in the Lord; and He reckoned it to him as righteousness. And He said to him, "I am the LORD who brought you out of Ur of the Chaldeans, to give you this land to possess it." He said, "O Lord God, how may I know that I will possess it?" So He said to him, "Bring Me a three year old heifer, and a three year old female goat, and a three year old ram, and a turtledove, and a young pigeon." Then he brought all these to Him and cut them in two, and laid each half opposite the other; but he did not cut the birds.

God never deserts His people. He sometimes delays, but He never forsakes. There is a promise of blessing that comes to everyone who will walk uprightly. Notice the eighth verse of this fifteenth chapter of Genesis: *He said, "O Lord God, how may I know that I will possess it?"* Abram does not put this test to God because he does not believe God or because he believes that God may fail him, but because it was the custom in those days for a person to give a pledge of the fulfillment of a promise. That is why he asked, *How may I know?*

God's answer to him is a very strange one. It is found in the verse that follows: *So He said to him, "Bring Me a three year old heifer, and a three year old female goat, and a three year old ram, and a turtledove, and a young pigeon* (Genesis 15:9). Thus, seated opposite the altar, we find Abram waiting. That is a wonderful illustration of faith in God. It is still early in the morning, and the offerings are before Him, but God does not speak. Still Abram believes God, and He counts it to him for a blessing. There was no sign of the acceptance of the sacrifice such as one would expect, but he does not waver. His faith is as firm as the rocks around him. Sarah may have ridiculed him, and the servants may have looked at him curiously, as if his mind was wandering, but Abram continued to wait. I am certain that one of the greatest blessings of his life came to him while he waited.

All of us have had our hours of waiting for the fulfil-
ment of God's promises. We have had sleepless nights.
We have climbed the hill hundreds of times to see if
there was a cloud the size of a man's hand, giving us
the sign of the coming of victory (1 Kings 18:43-44),
and the world has said that all our faith and hope was
in vain. But that was not the case at all.

This is when the spiritual life grows. It is also the
time when the unclean birds come to discourage us
and disturb us. Just as they hovered around the offering of Abram, so they soar above us, seeking to rob us
of the best things of our life – of all that would make
life worth living. However, it is possible for us to drive
them all away, just as we find Abram did in the text with
which we started: *The birds of prey came down upon the
carcasses, and Abram drove them away* (Genesis 15:11).

These offerings are the same as those commanded
to Moses, and if we put them all together, we have a
perfect illustration of the atonement of Jesus Christ
and of the power of His blood to make clean. I will
not consider the offerings in their order, but will give
them to you in this chapter as they have impressed
themselves upon my own mind.

I.

*He shall take the two goats and present
them before the LORD at the doorway of
the tent of meeting. . . . But the goat on
which the lot for the scapegoat fell shall be
presented alive before the Lord, to make*

> *atonement upon it, to send it into the wil-*
> *derness as the scapegoat.* (Leviticus 16:7, 10)

Because of the light shed upon the atonement, very few services in the Old Testament Scriptures are more interesting in the past, and more powerful as we study them in the present, than the offering of the goats. There were two in number, and in this there lies the very deepest thought of God in regard to sin. *What must I do to be saved?* (Acts 16:30) has been the heart cry of many poor lost souls, who no sooner utter it than the evil birds begin to fly about their heads, suggesting all sorts of answers to the question.

One whispers "Reform," and the poor tempted person makes an effort; but what a struggle he has, for he finds that when he has cut off one sin, the strength of it seems to go in the channel in which another has been flowing. He learns that reformation, even if it is complete (which it rarely is), only touches the present, and possibly the future, but never for a moment makes provision for one's awful past.

Another bird suggests that we should simply be good. One great evangelist says, "Stop being unkind." Another one, equally great, says, "Do right, and you will be a Christian."

With all due respect for these men who have been considered great, I submit that they are wrong; for one might stop being unkind today, but what about yesterday? And one may possibly do right tomorrow, but who is to make provision for the deeds of today?

Man's way has miserably failed. Let us now turn to God to seek the proper answer to the question.

The first goat was slain for the Lord, and this side of man's sin must never be forgotten. In the transgressions of man, God has been dishonored, His truth has been scorned, His authority has been set aside, His majesty has been insulted, His law has been broken, and His name has been despised. No reformation of man can ever make this wrong right. Thus, in the Old Testament, the goat was offered to meet God's demands, which were just, and to satisfy His holy law. And thus, in the New Testament, Jesus Christ came to suffer and to die.

There is much teaching today that magnifies the life of Jesus, but the clear teaching of the Word of God is that only by the shedding of His blood is there forgiveness of sins (Hebrews 9:22). *The blood of Jesus His Son cleanses us from all sin* (1 John 1:7). Much is said today about Jesus being a teacher, but He said Himself that the Spirit, when He is come, would teach us all things (John 14:26). Jesus Christ came to die – so that through His death, an avenue might be opened up for man to come back to his God and be reconciled forever unto God.

> Jesus Christ came to die so that an avenue might be opened up for man to come back to his God

But this is not all. The second goat was led forth with a scarlet cord around its neck. The hands of the priest were laid upon its head, the sins of the people were confessed, and then, by the hand of a suitable person, the scapegoat was led away into a land that was not inhabited. In this, it becomes a proper illustration of the Lord Jesus Christ. *The LORD has caused the iniquity of us all to fall on Him* (Isaiah 53:6), and He has carried our sins away, *as far as the east is from the west* (Psalm 103:12). It is an inspiration for us to know that when Jesus Christ died on Calvary, not only did He die to set us free from the penalty of sin in the sight of God, but by His death, we are set free from the power of sin in our own lives.

When someone becomes discouraged and finds that he by himself cannot keep from sin, the evil bird comes to whisper once again: "You need to expect it. You have been born with a tendency to sin. You have been cursed with a desire for sin. Your old nature is still with you."

If we are faithful students of our own nature and of the Word of God, we know and believe all this. However, this is no license to sin, for God's Word tells us, *If we confess our sins, He is faithful and righteous to forgive us our sins and to cleanse us from all unrighteousness* (1 John 1:9); that is, He will be faithful to Christ, who has carried our sin away.

> You simply have to hold up to Satan the expression "It is written," and he will be overcome.

Isaiah's picture in the fifty-third chapter of his prophecy is a picture of Jesus Christ as the scapegoat, carrying the weight of our sins through the wilderness.

For every evil bird that comes to discourage us or to discredit God's Word, there is a sure way by which they may be driven from us. The Word of God is our defense, and you simply have to hold up to Satan (whose agents these evil birds are) the expression "It is written," and he will be overcome.

II.

*Then the LORD spoke to Moses and Aaron,
saying, . . . the one who gathers the ashes
of the heifer shall wash his clothes and be
unclean until evening; and it shall be a
perpetual statute to the sons of Israel and
to the alien who sojourns among them.*
(Numbers 19:1, 10)

If someone were to give this passage of Scripture a
casual reading, he might find in it very little to grab
his attention. However, if he studies it carefully and
compares Scripture with Scripture, he will learn that
not only is it one of the most intensely interesting studies in all the Bible, but also that it sheds light upon the
gospel story and makes both plain and powerful one
phase of the work accomplished by our blessed Lord.

There was something in the color of the heifer, for
it was not allowable to have one single white hair. It
had to be all red. Certainly this is just a little hint that
in the sacrificial life and death of Jesus Christ, there
was not one single bright ray.

The offering must be without blemish. If there was
the smallest spot of weakness about it, it was to be
rejected. He was without *spot or wrinkle or any such
thing*, too (Ephesians 5:27). The Son of God, our Savior,
was absolutely perfect.

The red heifer was to be taken out of the camp, and
there put to death. Jesus was taken outside the city, and
He was crucified upon the green hill that we call Calvary.

When the heifer was burned, scarlet was cast into

the flames, which (I suppose) was used to typify the sins of Israel, for both theirs and ours are red like crimson, or scarlet. Cedar wood and hyssop were also cast in. The cedar was the grandest tree in the olden times, the king of the forest, while hyssop was the common, everyday plant that could be found outside the door of every cottage. Taking the hyssop on the one side and the cedar on the other, all nature would be included in the sweep. Surely there is a hint here as to the breadth of the atonement provided by Jesus Christ, and also a clear suggestion as to the power of Christ's blood to cleanse.

In the first twelve verses of the sixth chapter of Numbers, we have the law of the Nazarites. From this we learn that if the Nazarite defiled himself in any way, he must immediately be cleansed, or else would be out of fellowship with God. We see that if he is out of fellowship, the days of his uncleanness are lost with God. In other words, if any unconfessed or unforgiven sin is in our hearts or lives, we may be saved – we will not argue that question – but our time is lost. It counts for nothing with God, and we will one day be called to a strict account for this loss of time. How many Christians today are absolutely without power! Their voices were once heard in the prayer meeting. Their testimony once rang out clearly in the church. Their life in the home was without reproach. Yet today they have lost their testimony. It is when someone is in such a condition as this that the evil bird comes straight from hell to say to him, "Ah, yes! You once accepted Christ and made great professions. You once joined the church and gave much promise of usefulness. You were once prominent in the Christian world. But now this is past. You have lost it all, for your case is hopeless!"

I have been told that in the olden days, there was a Puritan pastor who every once in a while called the roll of the dead. He called the patriarchs by name, one by one, and then, standing silent in the pulpit, waited for an answer. The silence was voiceful. Then, looking at his congregation, he said, "Brethren, there is no response."

After calling these names, he would call the names of kings, the names of apostles, the names of famous historians, and the names of artists, scientists, inventors, and philanthropists. After the roll call, the same answer was given each time: "Brethren, there is no response. These men are dead."

I could call the names, too, if I would. Here is the name of one who was once the superintendent of a Sunday school, but who did not answer at the roll call. Here is another who once was an officer in the church, but his voice is silent. Here is another who was once honored in society for his professed faithfulness unto God, but there is no response to his name. And oh, the sadness! Here is another whose name was once a household word as an honored minister of the gospel, but there is no response to his name. What is the reason? It is because, like the Nazarite, they have come in contact with the dead. Their old sins have come up again, like bones from the grave, defiling their memory and robbing them of their power. It is because the very atmosphere they have been obliged to breathe, like ours, is against God and is in enmity to Christ. It is not easy to keep unstained from the world (James 1:27). The Jews considered every open vessel unclean.

But one is still left to us. Not long ago, there was a tragedy on one of the great western lakes in which a whole family was destroyed. A friend was asked to break the news to the only survivor of it. One daughter was left at home, and she had not yet heard of what was known in all the town. Everyone feared for her mental state after she was told of the great calamity. Gathering courage for her difficult task, the friend began: "I have something to tell you."

The girl at once suspected that something terrible was coming, and she asked, "Is it father? Where is he? And mother – where is mother?" The girl's heart stopped beating for suspense.

"Your mother is drowned, and your father too."

"But Tom, why is he not here? Is he gone too?"

"Yes, he too."

The poor girl could only whisper, "And Jennie – is she dead too?"

"Yes."

"And Ethel and Frank and the baby?"

"Yes, all gone."

"Are they all dead?"

"Yes, God help you. They are all gone."

A wild look came into the tearless eyes. Her friend was a devout woman, and so she said,

"But God is left."

The poor girl gave her a blinding look, and then burst into a flood of tears. That old-fashioned comfort that was the mainstay of our forefathers came to her aid. It saved the girl's reason by bringing to her aid her only Friend.

What was said to this brokenhearted girl, I say to you, and to all whose lives may have lost the peace of God. God is still love (1 John 4:8). He loves you, and having loved you, He will love you unto the end (John 13:1). His New Testament provision is a far better one than the old:

> *For if the blood of goats and bulls and the ashes of a heifer sprinkling those who have been defiled sanctify for the cleansing of the flesh, how much more will the blood of Christ, who through the eternal Spirit offered Himself without blemish to God, cleanse your conscience from dead works to serve the living God?* (Hebrews 9:13-14)

We do not need to stay out of fellowship or be deprived of power. God is love, and He will give us all things, if we simply fulfill His conditions.

III.

> *Then you shall take the other ram, and Aaron and his sons shall lay their hands on the head of the ram. You shall slaughter the ram, and take some of its blood and put it on the lobe of Aaron's right ear and*

> *on the lobes of his sons' right ears and on*
> *the thumbs of their right hands and on*
> *the big toes of their right feet, and sprinkle*
> *the rest of the blood around on the altar.*
> (Exodus 29:19-20)

Another part of the offering of Abram was the ram. This, like all the rest, sheds light upon the gospel, and the understanding of it is the secret of peace for many lives.

When the blood was sprinkled upon the ear and the thumb and foot, it was a sign that they were from then on to be separated from all worldly purposes. In this example, we get a deep lesson in regard to consecration. We have been told that we must forsake all for Christ, and some of us have done it. We have been counseled to give up the things that we have really enjoyed simply because they are questionable or contrary to the teaching of God's Word. Then when we have done this, the evil bird comes to us, saying, "You have forsaken these things, but what have you got in return?"

We frequently find people who stand in this position, who are of all people the most miserable. This is because they have only taken half the step. They have separated themselves from something, but have failed to consecrate themselves to anything. In other words, there are two sides to the doctrine of separation. We are to be separated *from the world*, but we are at the same time to be separated *unto Christ*, and the place that the world once filled is now to be occupied by Christ Himself.

It is to be noted that the blood was placed upon

the ear first. This is very significant to me. So many people get an idea that if they are converted, they must immediately do something for Christ, when in fact, service comes last. The blood placed upon the ear first teaches the lesson that we are to hear what the Lord has to say to us. If we could simply cultivate the habit of going alone each day and sitting still just to commune with God, what a source of strength it would be to us! God only tells His secrets to those who shut out the world, and thus come close to Him.

> God only tells His secrets to those who shut out the world, and thus come close to Him.

The blood was placed upon the hand next, from which I learn that not only are we to hear what God has to say to us, but we are to reach out and take what He offers. God has promised us the Holy Spirit. He is a gift. Reach out and take the gift.

The blood was placed upon the foot last. This may stand for service, but notice the divine order. We have reached a time when rules of service are hardly necessary, when we are certain that the methods adopted for soul winning must grieve the Holy Spirit. In fact, if one is to be used of God, he must certainly surrender to God and give Him the right of way in his life, and then service comes naturally and results are sure.

Dr. A. J. Gordon said that he started his church with all sorts of organizations, and that all of his time was required to keep them in order – and even then, he failed. But after a while, he swung away from these organizations to preach Christ, the life of self-surrender, and the fact that the Holy Spirit was to be the administrator of the affairs of the church. Now the organizations are few in number, but when his testimony was given before his departure, the church was filled with power and known throughout the world.

IV.

So He said to him, "Bring Me a three year old heifer, and a three year old female goat, and a three year old ram, and a turtledove, and a young pigeon." (Genesis 15:9)

We learn in one of the texts with which we started that part of the offering of Abram was that of a turtledove and a young pigeon. There is in this the very sweetest thought. These birds are bred plentifully in the East, and while one might not have been able to get a ram or a goat or a heifer, everybody could get a turtledove or a pigeon. They were for the poor. They were not to be divided.

We can understand how, in the study of the types, and also in the study of the gospel, evil birds would come to mystify us with these great doctrines. They might bring up the atonement and say, "Explain it if you can," and we cannot do it. They might submit to us the question of the divinity and the humanity of the Son of God, and we are perplexed in our minds, although we firmly believe it in our hearts. But no sooner do these evil birds come than we learn that everybody may have a turtledove or a pigeon to offer.

This somehow makes the truth plain to us, and the message very sweet.

It is said that a girl, known as Scotch Mary, went before the session of the Kirk in Scotland, but failed to pass the examination to join the church. She went a second time, and again failed. She could not answer the great questions of the church. She went a third time, with a similar result, and as she was turning away, the examiner stopped her in the manner typical of a Scottish minister, and she said to him, "I cannot answer your hard questions, but I know this: He died for me, and I can die for Him." He called her back, and the elders listened to her once again. Mary was at last admitted as a member, and she was a faithful one for many years after.

The turtledove and the young pigeon are types of the Holy Spirit. Two or three young men visited Washington recently and went into the National Museum. They passed a cabinet on which were the words: "The body of a man weighing 354 lbs."

"Where is the man?" someone asked. No one answered him. However, nearby was another cabinet containing an assortment of various items, including jars containing different kinds of fats, phosphates, lime, carbonate of lime, a few ounces of sugar, calcium, sodium, and other chemicals. Another section held a row of clear glass jars filled with gases, hydrogen, nitrogen, and oxygen. There was a square lump of coal, and more bottles separately labeled phosphorus, calcium, magnesia, and potassium. In a little jar was a fraction of an ounce of iron, and nearby was a lump of ill-smelling brimstone. The materials in these cabinets contained the disintegrated elements that would go to make up a person, but it was not a person; it needed the touch of God and His abiding presence to make these substances that the eye could see live, breathe, and become a thinking, willing man.

Thus does the Holy Spirit come, and thus must He ever come, to take the instrumentality of our churches and be the power behind them; to take the methods of our Christian workers and make the people understand that far beyond every man is the power of the Holy Spirit Himself. This plea is made so that every life may thus be yielded to His fellowship.

Far beyond every man is the power of the Holy Spirit Himself.

What is a yielded life?
  'Tis one at God's command,
For Him to mould, to form, to use,
  Or do with it as He may choose,
Resistless in His hand.

What is a yielded life?
  A life whose only will
When into blest subjection brought,
  In every deed, and aim, and thought,
Seeks just to do His will.

What is a yielded life?
    A life which love has won,
And in surrender, full, complete,
    Lays all with gladness at the feet
Of God's most holy Son.
        – W. A. G.

Chapter 8

The Bow in the Cloud

I set My bow in the cloud, and it shall be for a sign of a covenant between Me and the earth. – Genesis 9:13

At first, this may seem to be a strange text to choose for a gospel message, yet all the works of God are so wonderful that one only has to get the key to unlock the door leading into them to find them filled with sweetness and with help. The rainbow is no exception to this rule. It is hardly possible for someone to see the bow that spans the clouds after a storm without an exclamation of delight.

One would think that it would grow monotonous, for we have seen it so many times, but quite the opposite is true. Sunsets differ; they are as unlike as two things could possibly be. Indeed, it must be true that one is never like the other, but rainbows are always the same. Despite this, we are delighted as we look, and inspired as we study.

The first mention of a rainbow is in the text. It is not said that this is the first time the rainbow has appeared, for from the very nature of the case, it has always been in existence since the worlds began to be, but this is said to be the first use of it. The last mention of a rainbow is in Revelation 4:3: *He who was sitting was like a jasper stone and a sardius in appearance; and there was a rainbow around the throne, like an emerald in appearance.* You notice that the expression used is *around the throne,* and here for the first time we find a rainbow in a complete circle.

We have only seen half of it here, which is certainly an illustration of the fact that in this world, at best, we only get the half of things. We only get the half of truth. Take the great doctrine of the atonement: who is able to understand it? It is very helpful, though, to know that we are not obligated to understand it, but only to receive it. God is satisfied with it, and He fully comprehends it. When we stand with Him in glory, we will see the other half of the bow, and our hearts will rejoice. We only see the half of life here. At its best, it is a mystery. Over and over again, when we wanted to go to the right, we were compelled to turn to the left, and a thousand times because of our perplexities and trials, we have cried out, "How can these things be?"

However, we must learn the lesson that we must trust Him where we cannot understand Him. The day will come when we will be seated at His feet and will see the other half of the bow of our life, and we will know indeed that all things have worked together for good.

The last mention of the bow in Revelation tells us that it is to be like an emerald. This is certainly very strange, for we have never seen a green rainbow here. Six other colors must be added to it to make it complete. The color, however, is not without its significance. Green is the color that always rests the eye. It is for this reason that the hillsides, the waving branches of the tree, and the grass beneath our feet are so restful on a summer day. Is not this a hint that heaven is a place of rest as well as of beauty?

> We must learn the lesson that we must trust God where we cannot understand Him.

There are three primary colors in the rainbow: red, yellow, and blue. If you drop the red and put the yellow and the blue together, you have green as a result. Red is the color of suffering. Surely it is a hint as to the thought that when one passes through the gates of pearl, he leaves suffering behind him. There is to be no red mark in heaven. Christ finished His sufferings upon Calvary, and never a pain will meet Him again. We finish our sufferings, too, when we say good-bye to this weary road we have traveled, and the gate of heaven that shuts us in shuts suffering out.

The Cloud

We know what the cloud was for Noah (for this text that I have quoted has to do with him), and a cloud in Noah's day was not unlike the cloud of yesterday; but in the thought of the sermon, the cloud is sin.

It would make a person heartsick to read the history of sin. First, in the world, beginning with Adam, moving on to Noah, reaching the howling mob around the cross on Calvary, and coming down to the present day when the whole world seems to be touched with its power, the most terrible thing in the world is sin. Second, in the home, harming and attacking that which is a type of heaven, and wrecking that which God meant to be a safe vessel to carry us through the turmoil and strife that are always around us. Third, in our own hearts, giving us wrong conceptions of God and dragging us toward hell, even against our will. The darkest thing in all the world is sin.

The cloud does two things: 1) It obscures the sun, and 2) it compels us to see things in a false light.

It obscures the sun. The cloud of sin does the same thing. No one ever yet has had a true vision of Jesus Christ with the least particle of sin in his heart or life. *Blessed are the pure in heart, for they shall see God* (Matthew 5:8).

A poor fellow converted in one of the missions in Chicago, who was thought before his conversion to be hardly worth saving, was so wonderfully transformed that a committee waited upon him to find the secret of his changed life. He answered their question in just one sentence: "I have seen Jesus."

This vision always changes the life and transforms the character.

The cloud also compels us to see things in a false light. God made the works of His hands to be seen in the sunlight. We must not judge them under the cloud. A person can have no real conception of the Bible with the cloud of sin across his mind, for he would then certainly be prejudiced against the church.

Scatter the darkness that hovers over your mind, and the Bible will become to you the very thought of God, while the church will compel your admiration.

> A person can have no real conception of the Bible with the cloud of sin across his mind.

God Casts His Rainbow across the Cloud

To see a rainbow, three things are necessary. First, there must be a cloud. We certainly have that in the world's sin. Second, the sun must be shining. We have this condition met in the fact that *God is Light, and in Him there is no darkness at all* (1 John 1:5). Third, the rain must be falling. We have this in Isaiah 55:10-11:

> *For as the rain and the snow come down*
> *from heaven, and do not return there*
> *without watering the earth and making it*
> *bear and sprout, and furnishing seed to the*

*sower and bread to the eater; so will My
word be which goes forth from My mouth;
it will not return to Me empty, without
accomplishing what I desire, and without
succeeding in the matter for which I sent it.*

We might put it another way. First, in order that we may
be saved, we must acknowledge ourselves to be sinners.
This is the cloud. Second, we must have some idea of
God's hatred of sin. This is the light. Third, we must
be persuaded that He loved us and gave Himself for us
(Ephesians 5:2). This is the rain. With these conditions
met, the bow of promise spans the cloud of a sinful life.

The Seven Colors

If I would hold a prism in my hand and the light of
day would touch it, seven colors would at once be
refracted: red, orange, yellow, green, blue, indigo, and
violet. There has never been a rainbow in this world
in which these colors have not been seen in more or
less prominence. In my message now, the prism is the
cross and the light is God's truth. As it strikes this long
prism, it breaks up into seven colors. The seven colors
together give us the rainbow.

1. Forgiveness. *How blessed is he whose transgression
is forgiven, whose sin is covered!* (Psalm 32:1).

The word *forgiven* means "taken off." What a wonderful thought it is! What a load of sin we had to carry!
How it weighed us down! Day and night we went crying

aloud, saying, *Wretched man that I am! Who will set me free?* (Romans 7:24). Resolution never lifted it an inch. Reformation only seemed to make it heavier. Then Jesus came, stooped down, and whispered to us just one sweet word: "Forgiven!" When we realized it, the burden was taken off. To receive all of this, we only have to yield to God. Trying to make ourselves better only adds to the cloud and deepens our despair.

2. Cleansing. *Purify me with hyssop, and I shall be clean; wash me, and I shall be whiter than snow* (Psalm 51:7).

The little bunch of hyssop carries us back to the Passover night, when the lamb was slain and its blood collected. It was not said that one should take a brush, but a bunch of hyssop, and dip it in the blood and sprinkle the posts of the door. The most common thing that grew in the East was hyssop. It represents faith. One only had to step to the door of the cottage and stoop down to pluck a bunch of hyssop.

The most common thing in all this world is faith. We have faith in each other, whether we express it in this word or not. The faith that one has in his mother, in his father, in one's wife or husband, if turned toward Jesus Christ, would save his soul. It is one thing to be forgiven, but the color deepens and the truth sweetens when we know that because of the shed blood of Jesus Christ, we may be made clean. *The blood of Jesus His Son cleanses us from all sin* (1 John 1:7).

3. Justification. *He who was delivered over because of our transgressions, and was raised because of our justification* (Romans 4:25).

One might be perfectly sure of his forgiveness, might know that it meant that his sins were taken away and remembered no more, and might be confident of his cleansing, but there is the memory of the old life of failure that is always to him like a shackle when he tries to run to God. Justification is sweeter by far than anything we have yet learned. When Christ rose for our justification, He stood before God as a kind of a receipt (as John Robertson has said), and when God looks upon that receipt, He knows that the bill is paid.

> When one is justified before God, he actually stands as if he had never sinned.

> Jesus paid it all.
>> All to Him I owe.
> Sin had left a bitter stain,
>> He washed it white as snow.[5]

But justification is even better to me than this, for when one is justified before God, he actually stands as if he had never sinned.

4. Sins covered by the sea. *He will again have compassion on us; He will tread our iniquities under foot. Yes, You will cast all their sins into the depths of the sea* (Micah 7:19).

It is very comforting to know that there are some depths in the ocean so deep that they can never be sounded. Our sins must have gone as deep.

---

5 This is the refrain from the hymn "Jesus Paid It All," written by Elvina M. Hall (1820-1889).

There is also another thought of comfort: if a body is cast into the ocean where the waters are not very deep, then when the storms come and the ocean is in a fury, the storm, as if with giant hands, takes the dead body and casts it upon the shore. But there are depths in the sea so great that no storm that has ever yet swept across the face of the deep has stirred the waters. Thanks be unto God that our sins may be sunk so deep in the sea that they will never be cast up against us again. The color deepens and the truth grows sweeter still.

5. Sins removed. *As far as the east is from the west, so far has He removed our transgressions from us* (Psalm 103:12).

It has been proved that the distance from east to west could never be measured. This is certainly inspiring. However, there is something better for me than this in the fifth color, for when I am told that my sins are as far from me as the east is from the west, I know that the east and the west can never be brought together; nor can the saved sinner and his pardoned sins ever meet again.

6. Sins blotted out. *I have wiped out your transgressions like a thick cloud and your sins like a heavy mist. Return to Me, for I have redeemed you* (Isaiah 44:22).

A person cannot blot out his own sins. Some have tried it with their tears, and they have lost their reason. Some have attempted it by works of mercy, and they have given up in despair. But God can easily do it. Sins being blotted out may mean the same as for a person's account to be blotted out. I may have a bill charged against me on the books, but if on the opposite side is credited a sufficient sum of money to meet the indebtedness, it is blotted out. But the expression must mean more than this. It means that when one's sins are blotted out by God, they are as if they had never been.

7. Sins forgotten. This seems to be the climax of all. *None of his sins that he has committed will be remembered against him. He has practiced justice and righteousness; he shall surely live* (Ezekiel 33:16).

We have an idea that although our sins have been forgiven and we may have been justified, when the great day of judgment comes, we may be required to meet them all again. But this is not true. Once and for all He has put away sin by the sacrifice of Himself, and the sins of our lives will not again be mentioned to us.

God's Covenant

The rainbow was God's covenant then. Now God's covenant is His Word, and we may depend upon this Word. Notice the number of times God uses the expression *I will* in Exodus 6:6-8:

> *Say, therefore, to the sons of Israel, "I am the LORD, and I will bring you out from under the burdens of the Egyptians, and I will deliver you from their bondage. I will also redeem you with an outstretched arm and with great judgments. Then I will take you for My people, and I will be your God;*

and you shall know that I am the Lord
your God, who brought you out from under
the burdens of the Egyptians. I will bring
you to the land which I swore to give to
Abraham, Isaac, and Jacob, and I will give
it to you for a possession; I am the Lord."

He ever waits to fulfil the covenant that He has made with Christ concerning us. If we want to have the joy of salvation, we need only two things. First, we must believe God. No matter what our feelings may be, we must believe. Second, once we believe God, we must act as if we believe Him. The one gives us life, and the other gives us joy in life's possession.

> God ever waits to fulfil the covenant that He has made with Christ concerning us.

Chapter 9

Pilate's Question

Then what shall I do with Jesus who is called Christ? – Matthew 27:22

I t would not be possible for us either to understand or appreciate this passage of Scripture without studying that which immediately precedes it, and likewise that which follows. Next to Jesus Himself, the important character on the scene is Pilate, who asked the above question.

We never think of him without a shudder, because he is one of the men who came so very near to entering the kingdom of God; yet after all, he miserably failed. He came very near taking his place with Joseph of Arimathea and with Nicodemus. If, when he knew that Jesus was the Son of God, he had bared his own back to the smiters (Isaiah 50:6), or had gone himself to be crucified, there would have been no name in the early history of the church to outshine his. However, instead of being in the presence of God today, he is undoubtedly in the lost world.

When Jesus passed by the cross and went through the tomb of Joseph of Arimathea, made His way to the place of ascension, not far from Bethany, and left His wondering disciples, He took with Him into the skies His hands that had been pierced; His feet, through which the nails had torn their way; and His side, that had been thrust through with the spear, and against which the beloved disciple had leaned. In a word, He took with Him His body.

But there was one thing He left. When hanging on the cross, the blood came trickling down from His head, His hands, His feet, and His broken heart, and not only stained the rocks upon Calvary, but left its mark upon the world as well. Leaving His blood here, the world is today responsible for it. That same blood is upon both the world and men, either for their condemnation or for redemption.

There was a remarkable book that came across the seas some years ago bearing the title of *Letters from Hell*. It was written by Valdemar Adolph Thisted and had an introduction by George MacDonald, the celebrated Scottish preacher. In this book, there is a story of Pilate in the lost world stooping down to wash his hands in a running stream. He continues, it would seem, almost for ages, if time were measured as in this world. Someone touches him and says, "Pilate, what are you doing?"

Lifting his hands, which become red like crimson as soon as they leave the water, he cries out with a shriek that echoes and reechoes throughout the world of the lost, "Will they never be clean? Will they never be clean?"

Poor Pilate! His hands will never be clean, for the blood of the Son of God is on them for condemnation forever. He began to wash his hands when he said to the angry mob, *Take Him yourselves and crucify Him, for I find no guilt in Him* (John 19:6). He is still washing his hands today, but in vain.

There are special ways of treating texts of Scripture. One of the easiest ways is to take certain words in the verse and emphasize them, and make each word define the outline of the sermon. My text can be treated in this way.

> The person who says that he will neither accept nor reject Christ has rejected Him in the very position he takes.

What

The first word to emphasize would be *what*. Reading the text with this in mind, we find it saying, *Then **what** shall I do with Jesus?* The inference is that we must do something. We cannot be indifferent. The person who says that he will neither accept nor reject Christ has rejected Him in the very position he takes. There is no middle ground in this matter. We are either for Christ or against Him, and we must decide which position it will be.

Shall I do

The next words to emphasize would be *shall I do.* The particular part of the expression that is emphatic is the personal pronoun *I.*

Religion is a very personal matter, and judgment will be too. There is no one whose eyes will read this printed word who will not one day be called to an account for his rejection of the Son of God if he fails to acknowledge Him before men. Rich and poor, high and low, wise and ignorant – the question comes for all: *What shall I do?*

Then

The next emphatic word would be *then.* It might be used in two ways. We have made a choice between two things, and when we choose one, then it naturally follows that we must do something with the other. It is easy to understand that choosing one implies the rejection of the other. But it might also be taken as a word describing some future time, and I would like to think of it here as meaning, "Then what shall I do *in the day of judgment* with Jesus Christ?" When the moon will be turned into blood and the sun will be as black as the sackcloth of hair (Joel 2:31; Acts 2:20), and when the *elements will melt with intense heat* (2 Peter 3:10, 12) – **Then** *what shall I do?*

In the sixth chapter of Revelation, we read that in the last day, people will cry out and say to the rocks and hills, *Fall on us and hide us from the presence of*

Him who sits on the throne, and from the wrath of the Lamb; for the great day of their wrath has come, and who is able to stand? (Revelation 6:16-17). In the closing part of Revelation, though, we are told that there will be no rocks and no hills to fall upon the lost and shut out the vision of the face of the Son of God, and they must see Him whether they want to or not, Him whom they have rejected, Him from whom they have deliberately turned away.

Jesus

The next emphatic word is the name *Jesus. Then what shall I do with **Jesus?*** Jesus was His earthly name, and it described His earthly life. *You shall call His name Jesus, for He will save His people from their sins* (Matthew 1:21). His earthly life came to its climax in His sacrificial death upon the cross. To pay the penalty of sin, His life was given up, and if we fail to accept Him as a personal Savior, we deliberately take our stand with those who have nailed Him to the cross. When we stand before God, we will be called to an account for this greatest of all sins, for to reject the Son of God is to crucify Him again (Hebrews 6:6).

Christ

The last word to emphasize would be His anointed name, which is *Christ. Then what shall I do with Jesus who is called **Christ?*** As Christ, He stands at the right hand of God as our Mediator and Advocate. For fear that someone would say, "If I would become a Christian, I could not hold out," God seems to sweep away every false argument and false hope when He tells us that after we have accepted Him as Jesus, He becomes Christ for us and takes His stand at God's right hand, pleading for us in our weakness, and ever bringing to God's remembrance His atoning death so that our many sins may be washed away and forgotten.

Another outline has also been suggested as being a proper one to be brought out of this text. R. A. Torrey has made the suggestion that there are certain things that naturally depend upon what we do with Jesus. I will briefly mention these.

I. Our acceptance before God depends upon what we do with Jesus. *He who believes in Him is not judged; he who does not believe has been judged already, because he has not believed in the name of the only begotten Son of God* (John 3:18).

If we accept Jesus, God accepts us. If we reject Jesus, God rejects us. These are short sentences, but each one is worth a lifetime of study. The vilest sinner in the world who accepts Christ is immediately accepted by God. The most upright person who rejects Christ is instantly rejected by God. The moment we accept Him, we are justified from all things from which we could not be justified by the law of Moses. Justification is more than pardon, for in pardon and forgiveness there may still be the memory of sin, but when God justifies us,

> If we accept Jesus, God accepts us. If we reject Jesus, God rejects us.

He remembers against us our transgressions no more forever (Isaiah 43:25; Hebrews 8:12).

II. Our becoming children of God depends upon what we do with Jesus. *But as many as received Him, to them He gave the right to become children of God, even to those who believe in His name* (John 1:12).

There is a very harmful and deceptive kind of heresy making its way through the world today that declares there is such a thing as the universal fatherhood of God and the universal brotherhood of man. It states that God is the father of all His creatures, and that every man is my brother. This is certainly contrary to the Scriptures. We do not necessarily become children of God by the lives we live, by doing good, by reading the Bible, or by praying without ceasing, but we become God's children by regeneration. This is the work of the Holy Spirit, and it is worked in us the very moment we accept Jesus Christ as Savior by faith. It is not possible for us to come into this world in any other way than to be born into it, and it is not possible for us ever to enter the kingdom of God except by the new birth. This establishes us as children of God.

III. Our having peace depends upon what we do with Jesus Christ. *Therefore, having been justified by faith, we have peace with God through our Lord Jesus Christ* (Romans 5:1).

When we remember that peace is the opposite of confusion, strife, and unrest, we are able to see how great the blessing is that comes to us by accepting God's Son.

We do not think of peace as simply an emotion. It is not an experience, but it is that which comes to us with the presence of Christ. He is our peace (Ephesians 2:14), and no matter what a person's position may be in the world, if he has rejected Christ, or (in other words) if he has failed to accept Him, he must go forever throughout the world crying, "Peace, peace," but for him there can be no peace (Jeremiah 6:14).

IV. Our having joy depends upon what we do with Christ. *Though you have not seen Him, you love Him, and though you do not see Him now, but believe in Him, you greatly rejoice with joy inexpressible and full of glory* (1 Peter 1:8). We also remember the words of Jesus when He said, *These things I have spoken to you so that My joy may be in you, and that your joy may be made full* (John 15:11).

Joy is better than happiness. People of the world may have happiness, but only God's children possess joy. Happiness is that which happens to come to us, and those who lay hold upon it are dependent upon their circumstances and surroundings. Joy has nothing to do with circumstances or surroundings, but comes to us because of our faith in Him who ever lives to pour out upon His people His own presence and blessing.

V. Our having eternal life depends upon what we do with Jesus. *He who believes in the Son has eternal life; but he who does not obey the Son will not see life, but the wrath of God abides on him* (John 3:36).

By nature, we have the flesh with us, and we will always have it with us until we receive our redemption bodies. It is natural, therefore, that there should be a constant battle between the life of God that comes in regeneration and the old nature that is at enmity with God and always must be.

However, it is a great joy to know that every one of us may so surrender ourselves to Him who is our Life that the old nature will be put down and held in subjection, and we ourselves are more than conquerors (Romans 8:37).

> It is a great joy to know that every one of us may so surrender ourselves to Him who is our Life.

Finally, let me say that there are three sentences that should be written plainly before everyone who is to make this decision, or who fails to make it.

1. We must either accept Him or reject Him.

2. We must either let Him come into our hearts, or we must shut the door and keep Him out.

3. We must either confess Him or deny Him. *Everyone who confesses Me before men, I will also confess him before My Father who is in heaven. But whoever denies Me before men, I will also deny him before My Father who is in heaven* (Matthew 10:32-33).

There is no middle ground. May God pity us if today we turn away from Him, for it may be the last time!

Chapter 10

Now Peter

Now Peter was sitting outside in the courtyard. – Matthew 26:69

This is the masterstroke of the great artist in painting the picture of this child-hearted, wayward, generous, loving man whom we know as Peter. It is one of the shadows in the picture, but the shadows help us to more fully appreciate the light. It is a single sentence, yet we find in it the secret of a soul's downfall, the cause of the heartache of the Son of God, and a note of warning for God's people everywhere.

Peter was in a dangerous position. First of all, he was in a dangerous position because he sat in the presence of the enemy. In the first Psalm, the warning is given that we should not *walk in the counsel of the wicked, nor stand in the path of sinners, nor sit in the seat of scoffers* (Psalm 1:1), and this last is the most dangerous position of all. Poor Peter was sitting down.

He is also to be pitied because he *was sitting outside.* There is a circle within which every child of God must remain if he wants to have both peace and power. If in imagination we take a compass in our hand and set one point at the place where we would have the center, and with the other point describe the circle, we have the picture of the Christian life. The center of the circle is Christ, and the circle itself is described by prayer and Bible study and fellowship with the saints. To keep within this circle is to keep in touch with Christ. To sit outside is to be in danger, and poor Peter had stepped outside.

With all my heart, I love to study Peter. The sermon that has been greatly blessed to the people throughout the country is the one that bears the title "And Peter." This one is sent forth so that it may be a companion of that sermon and carry the name of "Now Peter."

I like him for his service. The first service that I can find that Peter ever rendered unto Christ is recorded in Luke 5:3: *He got into one of the boats, which was Simon's, and asked him to put out a little way from the land. And He sat down and began teaching the people from the boat.* I have an idea that just the way he pushed the boat out as the Master was standing in it made Jesus understand that there was something in him that would yet go far toward moving the world. Is it not true that much of the great work that we find about us today begins in just such a humble manner as the work of Peter did?

I like to study him in his writings. Some parts of the Bible should always be read in the sunlight. The beautiful story of Ruth, and the letter to the Philippians, are examples of this. Others are for the darkness. Peter's epistles would head this list. It is when we stand on the seashore at night that we see the phosphorescence of the waves. It is when we stand in the darkness and read Peter's precious words that we catch the best vision of the light that comes down from heaven and rests upon men.

I like to study him in his preaching, for it is just the kind that everybody should be able to do. You may say that his mighty sermon at Pentecost was simply a string of texts, but if you would say this was all that he said, we could reply, as we have said in another place, that it is all that Peter said that the Holy Spirit thought was worth recording.

I like him for his sincerity. You can read him with one quick look. He could not be a hypocrite. When he tried that once, no one would believe him. He generally thought aloud. While people sometimes admired him, frequently laughed at him, and generally criticized him, they always loved him.

I like him for his promptness. He was the first to enter the tomb so that he could see where the Lord lay.

I like him for his courage. He was not afraid to stand in the very midst of the enemies of Christ.

I like him for his intensity. It is true that he made mistakes, but the pendulum swung as far toward uprightness as it did toward failure.

I.

My text is to be read in connection with his denial, and thus we begin to appreciate the story even more. Christ had given him a warning when He said, *Simon, Simon, behold, Satan has demanded permission to sift you like wheat* (Luke 22:31), and again when He said, *The rooster will not crow today until you have denied three times that you know Me* (Luke 22:34). He warns us also.

The oak that goes down in the midst of the storm does so because throughout the long years, its heart has been eaten away by the worm. The soul of the child of God is never overthrown suddenly, and if it goes down, it is because it has steadily lost ground in matters that were considered too inconsequential to cause alarm. If you would fail tomorrow, you will undoubtedly find the cause if you look back on the history of today. The neglected Bible of today, the neglected prayer of today, and the neglected fellowship of today means the denial of tomorrow.

The soul of the child of God is never overthrown suddenly.

It is not to be forgotten that there were three denials. When Jesus was taken into the presence of those who were to condemn Him, Peter followed and wanted to go in too. It is said in John's Gospel that another disciple, who was known unto the high priest, had gone in with Jesus (John 18:15), and of course, this must have been John. They undoubtedly knew him at the door, and he passed through without question. When he saw that Peter was not in, he went to the door and secured his admission. I can just imagine how Peter must have walked up and down the court, now sitting, now standing, now trembling for his safety – for in those days, just as today, "conscience does make cowards of us all."[6]

The first denial was at the wicket gate. To the little girl that admitted him to the court he said, *I do not know Him* (Luke 22:57). He could have taken warning and gone back if he had only remembered the words of Christ, for he was just at the edge of the circle. One side meant peace, and the other side meant despair.

I do not doubt that someone reading these words has just passed through the wicket gate, turning away from a life of blessedness, and possibly has denied his Master for the first time. From the heart of the infinite Christ, a cry goes out to such a person: *Turn back, turn back . . . ! Why then will you die?* (Ezekiel 33:11).

The second denial was at the fire, when he sat with his enemies, and when he said with an oath, *I do not know the man!* (Matthew 26:74).

Sadly, many of us have gone through the wicket of

---

6   This is from William Shakespeare's *Hamlet*.

denial, and are today sitting with His enemies, hardly knowing how we reached the position. To all such people, the cry of God comes: *Come out from their midst and be separate* (2 Corinthians 6:17). The world has always been the enemy of the Son of God, and he who allows himself to be in touch with it in the least will deny his Master before he is aware of it.

The third denial was to the relative of Malchus (John 18:26-27), whose ear he had cut off in his supposed defense of his Master. For this attack upon his fellowman, he was undoubtedly answerable to the law, and possibly might have been tried and condemned if Jesus had not replaced the ear. The memory of Malchus stirred up all the terror imaginable in him, and before he knew it, the third denial was upon him. With repeated oaths and cursings he said, *I do not know the man!* (Matthew 26:74).

This is the denial that comes because of some unconfessed sin. It is unfortunate for the person who allows any sin to go without immediate confession! It will spring upon him some day like a tiger from the jungle, and will overthrow him before he can have time to call for help. Sin always downgrades in its tendencies, and he who denies Christ at the wicket gate will before long deny Him face to face.

II.

This text is also to be used in connection with the sufferings of Jesus. It may be good to give a brief account of His trial.

First of all, He appeared before Annas, the high priest, an account of which we read in John 18:19-22:

> *The high priest then questioned Jesus about His disciples, and about His teaching. Jesus answered him, "I have spoken openly to the world; I always taught in synagogues and in the temple, where all the Jews come together; and I spoke nothing in secret. Why do you question Me? Question those who have heard what I spoke to them; they know what I said." When He had said this, one of the officers standing nearby struck Jesus, saying, "Is that the way You answer the high priest?"*

It was a terrible thing for this man to strike Him in the face with an open hand; to strike Him before whom the angels veiled their faces; to strike Him to whom is sung, *Holy, holy, holy is the Lord God, the Almighty* (Revelation 4:8).

Do you notice that when they struck Him, He never shuddered? They could not hurt Him with any such blows as these. However, when we read, *Now Simon Peter was standing and warming himself* (John 18:25), this is a blow that makes the Son of God shudder and His heart grow sick.

The second part of the trial was His appearance before Caiaphas. Here, although false witnesses appeared against Him, He was perfectly silent:

> *But Jesus kept silent. And the high priest*
> *said to Him, "I adjure You by the living*
> *God, that You tell us whether You are the*
> *Christ, the Son of God." Jesus said to him,*
> *"You have said it yourself; nevertheless I*
> *tell you, hereafter you will see the Son of*
> *Man sitting at the right hand of Power,*
> *and coming on the clouds of heaven."*
> (Matthew 26:63-64)

Then they spat in His face (Matthew 26:67), but He never saw them. His eyes were blinded to His insults, but Peter in the presence of His enemies was a blow at His very heart. They smote him until, if He had been only man, He would have staggered in His weakness; but they might as well have struck a rock like Gibraltar and expected it to fall as to move Him with their blows. However, when Peter stood in the presence of those who were against Him, like one of them himself, it was a terrible blow at the Son of God.

The third part of the trial was before the Sanhedrin. He was led out from the court where He had seen both Annas and Caiaphas, and He passed through an outer court to another room where the Sanhedrin was to meet. As He passed, possibly near enough to reach out His hand and touch His disciple, suddenly He heard Peter say, *I do not know the man!* (Matthew 26:74).

He could forget the spitting of His enemies, the blows of those who hated Him, and the rods that had fallen upon Him in the hands of the angry multitude, but He could not forget Peter.

That which hurts Him the most in these days is not the sin of the unconverted, for He expects this, but He is most hurt by the sins of His own people for whom He suffered, died, and rose again.

There is an infinite amount of heartbreak in the words, *The Lord turned and looked at Peter* (Luke 22:61). No word of reproach fell from His lips, but simply an expression of sorrow was to be seen. Does He not look upon you today, and does He not awaken memories in your life – vows that you have broken and pledges that you have never kept?

> That which hurts Jesus the most in these days is not the sin of the unconverted, but the sins of His own people.

> Jesus, let Thy pitying eye
> Call back a wandering sheep.
> False to Thee like Peter, I
> Would fain, like Peter, weep.[7]

III.

Do not be discouraged. Man's usefulness frequently springs from his recovery from some sin. Out of Peter's fall came his first epistle. The best glimpse I have of the Savior's heart is that which comes when I think of His personal dealings with individuals. When I think of the God of Abraham, I think of one who strengthens His child under trial. The God of Jacob is

---

7   This is from a hymn by Charles Wesley (1707-1788) that begins with "Jesus, let Thy pitying eye."

my encouragement to believe that my old nature may be conquered and that my name may be changed from Jacob to Israel, the prince of God. The God of Elijah teaches me that prayer must be answered. The Savior of Thomas encourages me while in doubt. The Savior of Paul sustains me in my suffering. The Savior of Peter is the Restorer of the repentant.

Peter and Jesus met after the resurrection on the shore of the Sea of Tiberias (John 21). It is most significant that when he denied Christ, it was in the presence of the fire of coals in the court of the enemy. When the Son of God met him on the shore of this lake, there was a fire of coals burning there. I do not doubt that the entire story of his denial came rushing upon him. We will not know what was said in that interview until we hear it from Peter's own lips, but it is safe to say that all his sins were forgiven, and even the marks of his denial were taken away.

If you have denied this same Lord in your business, in your home, or in society, He waits to forgive and to forget, and He *is the same yesterday and today and forever* (Hebrews 13:8).

Chapter 11

A Vision of His Face

They will see His face. – Revelation 22:4

It is thought that the Apocalypse, or book of Revelation as it is more frequently called, was written around AD 95 to 97, and thus for nineteen hundred years, the Christian world has been living in the hope and inspiration of this text of Scripture. The glad cry of the faithful everywhere has been, *As for me, I shall behold Your face in righteousness; I will be satisfied with Your likeness when I awake* (Psalm 17:15).

I wish we could see Him now. We have had hints of His beauty and little glimpses of His glory, but oh, to behold Him! We are greatly indebted to the artists of the world for what they have shown us of their vision of His grandeur. *Christ before Pilate* was a painting so real that a little girl, when she looked upon it, wanted to be lifted up so she could untie His hands. Hoffman's *Christ in the Garden* is such a masterpiece that one cannot look upon it without having his emotions stirred to the very depths.

Paintings have certainly done their work. They have stirred the imaginations of the people. They have strongly impressed the beauty of His character upon hearts everywhere. They have focused the thoughts of men upon Him. They have drawn the Christian nearer to Him, and they have done much to stimulate fellowship with Him always. Indeed, some people have been won to Christ by simply looking upon them. Count Zinzendorf, founder of the Moravian settlement, said that the deepest impression that was ever made on his life came to him when looking upon a picture of the sufferings of Christ. He saw these words underneath: "I did all this for thee; what hast thou done for Me?"

Yet as valuable as they are, they are not to be relied upon because they are not ancient enough. The early Christians wanted to avoid any material presentation of a human Christ, and so it is that art as we have it today has passed through certain definite stages.

In the earliest age, Christ was presented by the use of symbols. The representation of the fish was to draw attention to Him who made men fishers of other men (Matthew 4:19). The drawing of a vine was to draw the attention to Him who said, *I am the vine* (John 15:5). The picture of the cross was supposed to affix the thoughts of the people upon Him who was its willing victim.

The second stage of art was the use of Old Testament types. In the picture of Moses striking the rock, one could see a representation of Christ, who said, *If anyone is thirsty, let him come to Me and drink* (John 7:37). In the sacrifice of Abraham, both the love of God in the gift of His Son and the love of the Son in the gift of Himself shine forth. In the three children in the fiery furnace, there is a perfect representation of the Son of God seen in the form of the fourth (Daniel 3:25).

In the third stage of art, New Testament allusions were used, and a shepherd became a picture of Christ, who was the *good shepherd* (John 10:11), the *great shepherd* (Hebrews 13:20), and the *Chief Shepherd* (1 Peter 5:4).

In the eighth century, men began to paint His likeness as they imagined it, but it is easy to understand that these representations could not be reliable because every trace of His physical appearance was lost. Not a syllable in the Gospels or the Epistles tells us how He looked when He walked upon the earth. Why is this? Surely the disciples had not forgotten His appearance. It may be for several reasons. First, because the first ages of the church were distinctly spiritual, and they would want to avoid anything that would make Christ even seem to be material. Second, they never thought of Him after His departure as the afflicted one or the suffering one, but they saw Him at the right hand of God in glory, and since they had no power to present a picture of Him there, so they had no inclination to present Him in His humiliation. Third, because they still felt His presence with them. They had no need to put His face upon canvas. I would a thousand times rather have the picture I carry around with me of Christ, which no artist has ever painted or ever can paint, which I could not describe to you in words even if I had the tongue of an angel. It is far beyond any earthly art. The early disciples must have felt this. Fourth, it may be that because when they saw Him after the resurrection, He was so different from what He was before that they could not paint the first picture, and they would not try to paint the second.

Yet we do know much about Him. It would not have been difficult for the author to tell how Stephen looked. We only have to read Acts 7:55, 60: *Being full of the Holy Spirit, he gazed intently into heaven and saw the glory of God, and Jesus standing at the right hand of God. . . . Then falling on his knees, he cried out with a loud voice, "Lord, do not hold this sin against them!" Having said this, he fell asleep.*

So it is with Jesus Himself. We have had some hints of His beauty in the legends of old. The story of Veronica tells of the handkerchief used to wipe His face as He went to Calvary, upon which the impression of His face was left, and which was to be seen as it was unfolded in the presence of Mary, His mother. This is a Roman Catholic story, and it has no foundation in fact.

There is also the story of Publius Lentulus, mentioned as the president of the people of Jerusalem, who is said to have written the following to the Roman Senate:

> There came one among us, tall in stature,
> beautiful in appearance, His hair wavy and
> crisp and falling down over His shoul-
> ders. His brow, broad, smooth and most
> serene. His face without spot or wrinkle
> or any such thing. His nose and mouth
> faultless. His beard abundant, and hazel-
> color like His hair. His eyes prominent and
> blue. In denunciation, terrible; in admoni-
> tion, calm and loving. He was never seen
> to laugh, but often to weep. His hands,
> beautiful to look upon. In speech, grave,
> reserved, modest. Indeed, He was fairer
> than all the sons of men.

All this is beautiful and interesting as a legend, but it is said that there was no such office as president of the people of Jerusalem to the Roman Senate, and that Publius Lentulus never lived.

Why all this absence of Christ in marble, and Christ upon the canvas? Why is it that the pen has never described Him so that we might reproduce His face? It certainly must all be of God. One reason may be in order that we might know that He belongs to the entire world, and not to any race of people in particular. If He were known to be white, the black man might feel that He was not in sympathy with him. If He were known to be black, the white man would certainly feel a barrier between them.

> Jesus belongs to the entire world, and not to any race of people in particular.

But as it is, He is Jesus, the Light of the World, and the Caucasian, the Mongolian, and the African can all say together: "Fade, fade each earthly joy; Jesus is mine."[8]

However, there are phrases of Scripture that seem to give us hints that should not be passed by silently.

His face set to go to Jerusalem

When the days were approaching for His ascension, He was determined to go to Jerusalem (Luke 9:51). He steadfastly set His face to go to Jerusalem.

He loved this city of Jerusalem, but at the time He went toward it, it was a city of shadows, and every step He took was into the deepening shadow of Calvary's cross. I do not need to describe His going. He was like a conqueror. In the very way He walked the streets of the city and the highway of the land He loved, He was filled with courage, and when He beheld the city, He wept over it (Luke 19:41). Take this as a picture, and there is nothing finer in art. Take it as a sentiment, and there is nothing deeper in human emotion. Take it as a revelation of God, and no one needs to be afraid of Him.

Philosophy may speculate about Him and try to reconcile His two natures; theologians may attempt to define Him as being infinite, eternal, and unchangeable; but the common man grows confused, and all that he can say is that the One to whom he has given his soul is the Son of God, who was divine enough to go to Jerusalem in the very face of death, and human

---

8   This is the beginning of a hymn written by Catherine Bonar (1821-1884), wife of Horatius Bonar.

enough to be blinded with His tears as He looked upon the city. He knew all about the suffering of Jerusalem from all eternity, yet He went on. When He ate the Passover and spoke of the one who would betray Him, He knew what was coming, and still He went on. When Pilate mocked Him, He knew it was only the foreshadowing of the sufferings of the cross, but still He went on. When He endured the pain of the scourging, He knew that this was only the beginning of agony with which the pain of the cross was not to be compared because it was so great, yet He went on. The world has never seen such a conqueror as the Son of God, who died so that we might live (2 Corinthians 5:15).

> The world has never seen such a conqueror as the Son of God, who died so that we might live.

His face in the dust

Then Jesus came with them to a place called Gethsemane, and said to His disciples, "Sit here while I go over there and pray." And He took with Him Peter and the two sons of Zebedee, and began to be grieved and distressed. Then He said to them, "My soul is deeply grieved, to the point of death; remain here and keep watch with Me." And He went a little beyond them, and fell on His face and prayed, saying, "My Father, if it is possible, let this cup pass

from Me; yet not as I will, but as You will."
(Matthew 26:36-39)

We read in Matthew 26:30 that when they had sung a hymn, they went out. How simple, yet how profound the meaning! There had never been such a going out before, and there never has been such a going out since. From the supper, He made His way with the faithful few to Gethsemane, where the agony was so great that Gethsemane has stood for suffering ever since.

My Father, if it is possible, let this cup pass from Me (Matthew 26:39). I wonder what the reason was for such a cry. Someone has said it was because He was about to be branded as a sinner, treated as a sinner, and put to death as a sinner, and it was His horror of sin that squeezed the cry from His soul. Yet we have trifled with it, and sin has always been the same. It still is today, and will be until the end of time.

Dr. Gregg tells of a story in *Foxe's Book of Martyrs* where a Christian was to die a most horrible death. He was to be placed in a sack that was nearly completely filled with venomous reptiles. As he looked at it, he said, "I can stand this, for Jesus's sake." Yet when they put him in the sack, and he felt the first touch of the reptiles upon his face, he gave a shriek of agony that could not be described.

It is said that no one ever really knows what prayer is until he learns by the Spirit to put into practice this one offered in Gethsemane. It is not the kind that is offered to the congregation or that is said at the bedside before we close our eyes in sleep. It is the kind that is crushed out of us. It is the cry of the Syrophoenician woman: *My daughter is cruelly demon-possessed* (Matthew 15:22). It is the cry of Jesus in Gethsemane: *My Father, if it is possible, let this cup pass from Me.*

You say, "What! His Father, and He had all His suffering?"

Yes, He was His Father still – and yours also. In the midst of an agony that may have almost broken your heart, you might have cried, "My Father!" When there was not any hope in your life, you might have whispered, "My Father!" And if the cry had come from the heart, you would have gotten as quick a response: *Cease striving and know that I am God* (Psalm 46:10).

His face spit upon

But there is still another picture of His face in the New Testament:

> *The high priest stood up and said to Him, "Do You not answer? What is it that these men are testifying against You?" But Jesus kept silent. And the high priest said to Him, "I adjure You by the living God, that You tell us whether You are the Christ, the Son of God." Jesus said to him, "You have said it yourself; nevertheless I tell you, hereafter you will see the Son of Man sitting at the right hand of Power, and coming on the clouds of heaven."*

*Then the high priest tore his robes and said,
"He has blasphemed! What further need do
we have of witnesses? Behold, you have now
heard the blasphemy; what do you think?"
They answered, "He deserves death!"*

*Then they spat in His face and beat
Him with their fists; and others slapped
Him, and said, "Prophesy to us, You
Christ; who is the one who hit You?"*
(Matthew 26:62-68)

Have you noticed how quiet He was during all the mocking and the scourging? It must have been because of the Gethsemane experience. There are scenes in our lives that make talk a sacrilege. When you came back from following your child to the grave, or after you reached your home after being at the newly made grave of your mother, not a word was spoken. The house was as still as the tomb where they rested.

A night with God would have the same effect. They may spit upon Him and strike Him, but He does not feel it, for while He walks the earth, He lives in heaven. Paul found this out:

*I know a man in Christ who fourteen years
ago – whether in the body I do not know, or
out of the body I do not know, God knows
– such a man was caught up to the third
heaven. And I know how such a man –
whether in the body or apart from the body*

I do not know, God knows – was caught
up into Paradise and heard inexpressible
words, which a man is not permitted to
speak. (2 Corinthians 12:2-4)

Yet in fact, Paul was lying at the gate of Lystra. People thought he was dead. His back was bleeding. His whole body was bruised. It is a possible thing for us to be transfigured by the power of God and become insensible to every earthly experience. Just as when the hell-hounds were let loose against Jesus Himself, and they smote Him and spit upon Him, they never touched Him.

It is a possible thing for us to be transfigured by the power of God and become insensible to every earthly experience.

His face hereafter

We have hints as to what He is to be like in the hereafter. *For God, who said, "Light shall shine out of darkness," is the One who has shone in our hearts to give the Light of the knowledge of the glory of God in the face of Christ* (2 Corinthians 4:6).

We are told how He will appear to the sinner: *For the great day of their wrath has come, and who is able to stand?* (Revelation 6:17). There was a time when they covered His face as they smote Him: *Some began to spit at Him, and to blindfold Him, and to beat Him with their fists, and to say to Him, "Prophesy!" And the officers received Him with slaps in the face* (Mark 14:65). But not now.

His eyes pierce right through His beholders, and

their unforgiven sins pass by in terrible procession. Hear the cry of the lost soul: *They said to the mountains and to the rocks, "Fall on us and hide us from the presence of Him who sits on the throne, and from the wrath of the Lamb"* (Revelation 6:16).

Then I saw a great white throne and Him who sat upon it, from whose presence earth and heaven fled away, and no place was found for them (Revelation 20:11). This passage gives another touch to the picture, and what a change there is! Once there was in that face that which brought little children to Him and made women love Him; now the very earth and the heavens have fled away from Him. *For the eyes of the Lord are toward the righteous, and His ears attend to their prayer, but the face of the Lord is against those who do evil* (1 Peter 3:12). God's words are always true. *He who has ears to hear, let him hear* (Matthew 11:15).

We are told just a little as to how He will appear to the saint: *For You will not abandon my soul to Sheol; nor will You allow Your Holy One to undergo decay. You will make known to me the path of life; in Your presence is fullness of joy; in Your right hand there are pleasures forever* (Psalm 16:10-11). We have hints of this joy here. We have felt this pleasure because of His fellowship in this world. We have had these experiences, which have been like single notes dropped from the songs of heaven. But they will be gathered all together there in one grand anthem of praise, and we will be filled with the peace of God forevermore.

We will see Him

We also have some hints as to how this vision will affect us when we see Him. John said, *I fell at His feet like a dead man* (Revelation 1:17). It is supposed that the vision was so startling and the face was so sublime that just as people in this world are overpowered because of some wonderful experience, so John fell before Him in the skies.

The transfiguration scene is another representation.

> *Six days later Jesus took with Him Peter*
> *and James and John his brother, and led*
> *them up on a high mountain by themselves.*
> *And He was transfigured before them;*
> *and His face shone like the sun, and His*
> *garments became as white as light. And*
> *behold, Moses and Elijah appeared to them,*
> *talking with Him. Peter said to Jesus, "Lord,*
> *it is good for us to be here; if You wish, I*
> *will make three tabernacles here, one for*
> *You, and one for Moses, and one for Elijah."*
> (Matthew 17:1-4)

Peter said, "Let us live here forever." In this, he was simply expressing the longing of every Christian heart that beat after his; and what Peter longed for, God has promised to give us. Jesus at the transfiguration is an exact picture of Jesus as He stands in glory, and as we will see Him in eternity.

J. Wilbur Chapman – A Brief Biography

J. Wilbur Chapman was an American evangelist, pastor, and author who was born on June 17th, 1859, in Richmond, Indiana. He grew up in a devout Christian family and attended local schools. Chapman became a born-again Christian at a young age and felt called to the ministry.

After completing his studies at Lake Forest College and Lane Theological Seminary, Chapman began his pastoral ministry in 1882 in Indiana. He served as a pastor in several churches before moving to Philadelphia in 1890, where he became the pastor of the well-known Bethany Presbyterian Church.

During his time at Bethany Presbyterian Church, Chapman's ministry gained widespread attention. He was a dynamic preacher who emphasized the importance of personal salvation and the need for Christians to live a holy life. He also believed in the power of prayer and often encouraged his congregation to pray for the salvation of others.

Chapman's evangelistic efforts were not limited to his own congregation. He traveled extensively, preaching at revival meetings and other events across the country. In 1895, he organized a series of evangelistic campaigns in Philadelphia, which drew large crowds and resulted in many conversions.

In 1903, Chapman resigned from his position at Bethany Presbyterian Church to devote himself full-time to evangelistic work. He joined forces with gospel singer Charles Alexander, and the two began a series of successful evangelistic campaigns across the United States and abroad.

Chapman's preaching style was characterized by his passionate delivery and his emphasis on the need for personal salvation. He often used anecdotes and illustrations to convey his message, and his sermons were known for their clarity and simplicity.

In addition to his preaching, Chapman was also an author. He wrote several books on the Christian life, including *And Peter, The Secret of a Happy Day*, and *The Life and Work of D. L. Moody*. He also edited several books, including *The Gospel According to Christ*, a collection of sermons by prominent pastors.

Chapman's family life was not without difficulty. In May 1882, he entered into the bonds of matrimony with Irene Steddom. Not long after, in April of 1886, their daughter, Bertha Irene Chapman, was born. Sadly, Irene Steddom Chapman passed away in the same month. After some time had passed, Chapman remarried on November 4, 1888, to a woman by the name of Agnes Pruyn Strain. Together they had four children, but tragically lost their son Robert during infancy. The surviving children were John Wilbur Jr., Alexander Hamilton, and Agnes Pruyn. However, on June 25, 1907, Agnes Pruyn Strain passed away. The, on August 30, 1910, he married Mabel Cornelia Moulton. This was his third and final marriage.

Chapman's evangelistic campaigns with Charles Alexander were highly successful, drawing large crowds and resulting in numerous conversions. Their partnership lasted for more than a decade, and they traveled to countries such as Scotland, England, and Australia, where they preached to large audiences.

In addition to his evangelistic work, Chapman was also a prominent leader in the Presbyterian Church. He served as the moderator of the General Assembly of the Presbyterian Church in the United States in 1912 and was a strong advocate for Christian education.

Sadly, Chapman's ministry was cut short when he died suddenly on December 25, 1918, while on a speaking tour in New York City. His death was a great loss to the Christian community, but his legacy lived on through his writing and preaching.

Chapman was a leading figure in the early 20th-century revivalist movement in America. He was known for his passion for the Gospel and his emphasis on the need for personal salvation. His dynamic preaching and evangelistic campaigns drew large crowds and resulted in numerous conversions.

Chapman's influence extended beyond his own ministry. He mentored several prominent pastors and evangelists, including Billy Sunday, who went on to become one of the most famous evangelists of the early 20th century.

Today, Chapman's legacy lives on through his writing and the numerous pastors and evangelists he influenced. His emphasis on the importance of personal salvation and the need for Christians to live a holy life continues to inspire Christians around the world.